BUSH AGLOW

The author of this book was born in Terre Haute, Indiana. His education was received at the Bradley Polytechnic Institute, William Jewell College, and-in post-graduate courses-Leland Stanford University and the University of Southern California. Grand Island College gave him the divinity doctorate in 1929. From 1919 to 1924 he was pastor of the First Baptist Church of Riverside, California; from 1924 to 1931, of the First Church of Phoenix, Arizona. He has been a general evangelist and pulpit supply since 1940. Doctor Day began his literary career when a high school student as a reporter for the *Terre Haute Gazette,* and in the years since he has continuously written for publication. His "Beside the Golden Gate" column in *The Baptist* attracted much attention and was widely quoted. In 1934, Doctor Day's biography of Spurgeon, with the title *The Shadow of the Broad Brim,* was issued from The Judson Press.

BUSH AGLOW

"And the angel of the Jehovah appeared in a flame of fire out of the midst of a bush" (*Exodus*).

"I do not know anything America needs more today than men and women on fire with the fire of heaven: not great men, but true honest persons God can use" (D. L. M.).

BUSH AGLOW

The Life Story of Dwight Lyman Moody
Commoner of Northfield

By RICHARD ELLSWORTH DAY
Author of "The Shadow of the Broad Brim"

CROWN PUBLICATIONS

POWELL, TN

BUSH AGLOW

Copyright © 2008
Crown Christian Publications
Powell, Tennessee 37849

ISBN: 978-1-58981-129-4

Cover design by Stephen Troell
Layout and design by Joshua Tangeman

Printed in the United States of America

To

Miriam Elim Washburne
Who Intrusted Me
With the Washburne Collection
and

To
James Washington Graves
Who Illustrated Both
This Book and
"The Shadow of the Broad Brim"

CONTENTS

CHAPTER   PAGE

Author's Apology..1

So We Went Scouting..5
(SUMMER of 1935)

I. King Arthur's Yeomen in the
   Connecticut Valley.....................................15
   (1635-1828)

II. Squakeag Changes Its Name............................23
    (1669-1937)

III. Berkshire Madonna...................................33
     (1805-1896)

IV. Presumption Heads Up Toward the
    City of Destruction...................................47
    (1837-1854)

V. But Is Overtaken by the King..........................57
   (1854-1856)

VI. Westward, Ho!..67
    (1856-1860)

VII. Mr. Shoe Salesman Buckles on the
     Sword of Evangel....................................77
     (MARCH, 1860)

CONTENTS

CHAPTER   PAGE

VIII. Christiana Delays Not to Join the
        Progress......................................87
        (1843-1903)

IX. Pilgrim Walks in the Flesh......................103
        (1860-1871)

X. And His Works Become Bondage..................119
        (1860-1871)

XI. Till a Holy One Gives Him an
        Accolade of Fire................................127
        (NOVEMBER, 1871)

XII. The Holy One Greatly Enriches His
        Panoply......................................141
        (1871-1873)

XIII. He Is Joined by a Man with a
        Melodeon....................................155
        (1840-1873)

XIV. And the Church Begins to Sing!..................169
        (1873-1908)

XV. The World Turns Aside........................183
        (1873-1879)

XVI. He Continually Looks at His Scroll...........197

XVII. And Derives Abiding Convictions................211

XVIII. He Repairs to the Arsenal for His
        Arrows......................................221

CONTENTS

CHAPTER   PAGE

XIX. He Sets Up an Inquisition of Grace..............237

XX. Pilgrim Takes Up a Trowel...........................251
(1879-1899)

XXI. The Sword and the Trowel..........................269
(1879-1899)

XXII. He Groweth Much Heavenward....................277

XXIII. And Is Compassed About by a Cloud
of Witnesses.....................................289

XXIV. He Goes Up to Jerusalem...........................299
(APRIL 15-25, 1892)

XXV. And Copies Pentecostal Strategy................309
(MAY 1-OCTOBER 31, 1893)

XXVI. And Comes to the Gates of Glory................323
(DECEMBER 22, 1899)

LIST OF ILLUSTRATIONS

OPPOSITE
PAGE

The Grandmothers...22

Berkshire Madonna...32

The Birthplace...46

(Per Elizabeth Clapp Moody)

Presumption at Seventeen...56

Chicago of the Fifties...66

Mr. Shoe Salesman...76

Christiana...86

Pilgrim and the Man with the Melodeon.........................154

The Houses of Pilgrim's Trowel.....................................250

The Commoner of Northfield.....................................276

Winter View of Birthplace.....................................322

PREFACE

———•◆•———

D.L. Moody was a man mightily used of God. Reading of his love for Christ and his passion for the souls of men will stir you to have greater devotion to the Lord Jesus Christ.

Everyone who seeks to bring others to Christ will be helped and encouraged by this book.

This classic will stir your heart to follow Christ and fish for men. This is must reading for every soul winner!

Clarence Sexton
Acts 5:42

Clarence Sexton
Founder and President of Crown College

AUTHOR'S APOLOGY

I find that men (as high as trees) will write
Allegory-wise, yet no man doth them slight
For writing thus; then so will I!
Would'st thou remember
From New Year's day to the last of December?
Then read my fancies, they will stick like burs.
Would'st thou see
A man i' th' clouds, and hear him speak to thee?
Would'st know just how he runs and runs
Till he unto the Gate of Glory comes?
Would'st thou be in a dream and yet not sleep?
Would'st thou in a moment laugh and weep?
O, then come hither,
And lay my book, thy head and heart together.

—*John Bunyan, "Pilgrim's Progress."*

*　　*　　*

Now this is to be the Chronicle of a servant of the King, whose life and labors are set forth in this short, simple word,

My Human Best, Filled with the Holy Spirit.

—*Sketch Book.*

Author's Apology

Now it came to pass that an horror of great darkness fell upon me. For, seeing the Bride of Christ having ashes in place of beauty, I had boasted, *My prowess shall rescue her!* Then I found out what the Book meaneth where it saith, The Lord hath not pleasure in the legs of a man.

While I did much grieve over this state of affairs, the report kept coming of a rude, unlettered one who turned the world upside down for his Lord. So Deborah and I went scouting wherever he had been, always asking, *How did he do it?* And, lo! a serviceable annal grew in my *Sketch Book*.

*   *   *

Centuries ago, ship-loads of King Arthur's Yeomen moved into the wilderness of the Connecticut Valley and sturdily set up the pleasing village of Northfield in an Indian place called Squakeag. The person of whom I am to write was born in the line of these yeomen, and his mother was a Berkshire Madonna. The Young King, by way of setting forth His rule not by might nor by power, swiftly overtook this heavy country fellow upon his leaving home, placed in his hand that of a lovely Christiana, encouraged him to wield Evangel's sword, and then touched him with Fire.

Our Pilgrim was then joined by a young companion, armed with no greater weapon than a melodeon! Together they set out upon a quest to King

Arthur's Land. They seemed most humble in person. But lo! in a few days the world perceived anew the ancient miracle of the Angel of the Lord appearing in a flame of fire out of the midst of the bush; and it turned aside to see the great sight.

Behold, it maketh a fair tale to mark how the Holy One gave unto Pilgrim the engines of war; a Scroll upon which he did continuously look; Honest Arrows for his quiver; a Sword for his right hand, a Trowel for his left; and An Inquisition of Grace, whereby Stricken Sinners were transmuted into Steadfast Saints. By reason of the heavenly in him so constantly advancing, he was compassed about by a Cloud of Witnesses. Toward the end of his journey, he copied Pentecostal Strategy and thereby did his greatest works. It seemed a sad loss for the world when his King led him at last through the Gates of Glory. But my eyes have often opened their fountains at the reading of little messages I'm sure he left for such as me:

"The days of our Lord's power shall come again! Lo, to this end He doth require, more than anything in the world, men and women on fire with the Fire of Heaven; not great men, but true, honest persons He can use!"

So We Went Scouting
(Summer of 1935)

I will therefore draw back the veil, and show my much honored friend in his most secret recesses, that the world may see what those springs were, from which issued that clear, permanent, and living stream of wisdom, piety and virtue, which so apparently ran through all that part of his life which was open to public observation.
-Phillip Doddridge, "Life of Col. James Gardiner."

So We Went Scouting
(Summer of 1935)

Here is an item deserving a fixed place in the Litany of Gratitude:

For that refreshing which comes to Man-Soul, from a centennial re-study of Christian Great Hearts–Good Lord, we thank Thee!

In ordinary times, Biography's life-giving waters remain like treasures of snow, locked on the lofty shelves of libraries. A few hardy ones only, climb high and drink, and live. But, let a hundredth anniversary draw nigh! Lo, the dramatic facts of Some Ancient Valiant rush with vernal power over human thinking. Centennial psychology is surely one of God's attending angels through whom He is glorified.

The one-hundredth anniversary of the birth of Dwight Lyman Moody will come like springs in the desert for an age like this. That far-off Sunday morning, February 5, 1837, was marked by a New England blizzard, roaring across the treeless pasturelands bordering Northfield, Massachusetts. A lonely house, brutally pioneer, newly built and unpainted, lifted its clapboard siding to shield a young mother, bringing back her sixth child from the Valley of Anguish. A few days later, when a thin winter's sun lighted the snowy New England wilderness, she wrote in her Bible:

DWIGHT L. RYTHER MOODY
Was born Feb. 5, 1837. Sunday.

That very Bible, lying for months on my study-table here Beside the Golden Gate, has allowed me to company with angels. Over and over, as I reverently touched it, romantic movements flooded the imagination. I have watched one of history's refreshing incredibles–a lowly lad rise to a world figure; an exploit of such transforming consequence, that, as it were a type, the very impoverished pastureland around his birthplace changed to the forested glory of the Northfield Seminary Campus; and the barren nob of a hill just behind the house became to Christian pilgrims that Sylvan Zion called Round Top.[1]

But the first studies in this Life of Moody proved a disagreeable experience. For long time, weaving the pattern of *The Shadow of the Broad Brim,* I lived with Charles Haddon Spurgeon. To go abruptly from Spurgeon to Moody seemed like passing from Sierra Glory to Nebraska prairie. The plain, almost monotonous endowment of Moody, over against the genius of Spurgeon, made me despair of ever finding an adequate biographer's enthusiasm. Then suddenly came eyes to see that for those of us who must go through life as Poor Ordinaries, the story of the Commoner of Northfield has even higher value than that of the Heir of the Puritans.

[1]Adoniram Judson Gordon, August, 1893: "I was here at Northfield Seminary when the first building stood alone; and this field where we now stand was a rough and stony pasture."

Here, in the life of Moody is a divine apologetic, putting hope into our one-talent lives by proving endowment and advantage to be, in God's sight, small as the dust of the balance; that my uttermost for His Highest must never be an inventory of genius, but a program of consecration; that Faith's greatest romance in every age is a fresh proving that

> The world has yet to see what God will do with and for and through and in and by the man who is fully and wholly consecrated to Him.

Such a thesis finds an ideal exhibit in D. L. Moody. It will be to thousands of others, as it has been to me, sweet surgery to abide for hours, reproved and ashamed, before his White Consecration; to become convinced that our beleagured age stands in need, not so much of ten-talent men as God-conquered commoners.

But such a thesis has curious power to play subconscious pranks, as, for instance, a sustained depreciation of Moody by way of building a case. That would be unfair. Moody stands before us today as ruggedly winsome as his Berkshire Hills. But, after honest appraisal, there yet remains a baffling chasm between what he *was* and what he *did*; a chasm which may be bridged by one word only—God!

Let me respectfully present a biographer's credentials. Long search has put upon my shelves a practically complete bibliography, all the way from Daniels' excellent volume of 1875, Torrey's firebrand, Jessie McKinnon's spiritual portrait, to Erdman's simple classic–an even one hundred references.[2]

By purchase, loan, and gift, these source materials have come together, a very large collection. Eye witnesses also have greatly aided me, such as: Minnie Holton Callendar, the grand old woman of the Holton Homestead; William Norton; Dr. James Martin Gray; Dr. H. A. Ironside; Dr. Charles G. Trumbull; Mr. Samuel E. Walker of Northfield; Dr. Curtis Lee Laws; Mrs. Norman Perkins Wood, widow of D. L.'s beloved physician; and a host of others.

Then Deborah and I went forth on a wide quest in the summer of 1935, driving through thousands of miles in a shining new chariot from Detroit. We slept by deliberate choice on mountain slopes, brook sides, river meadows, just to be near where Moody had been, and to see the birds, the trees and the verdant New England hills he loved. We walked the summer-heated streets of great cities, following as best we could where he lived, and labored and prayed. The staffs of great institutions, as the Chicago Historical Society, gave their personal attention in the exacting search for accurate detail. Nor do we wish to forget the profit derived from hours spent in the old Northfield Cemetery, literally feeling out on ancient, leaning, black headstones detail to be had nowhere else.

[2] W. H. Daniels, *D. L. Moody and His Work*; R. A. Torrey, *Why God Used D. L. Moody*; Mrs. Peter McKinnon, *Recollections of D. L. Moody*; Charles Rosenbury Erdman, *D. L. Moody, His Message For Today*.

But the author's summum bonum is the Washburne Collection, an amazing treasury of relics of D. L. Moody, patiently gathered by his youngest sister, Mrs. Franklin Bryant Washburne (Elizabeth Clapp Moody) through a period of more than sixty years. I am deeply indebted to Miss Miriam Elim Washburne, daughter of Mrs. Washburne, of Racine, Wisconsin, who loaned this collection to me as a trust during the period of research. Indeed, it should be said that I conceived the writing of *Bush Aglow* as a companion biography to *The Shadow of the Broad Brim,* then abandoned the idea owing to the closely guarded copyright materials on Moody's life. After the project was dropped, Miss Washburne made possible its resumption, indeed urged it, by putting at my disposal the entire collection. This unexpected good fortune not only made quotation from other source material unnecessary, but brought such a flood of new light as to give this book the quality of an entirely fresh interpretation, even to the illustrations, selected from a great collection of unpublished daguerreotypes, pictures, etc.

Mrs. Washburne, widow of Dr. Franklin Bryant Washburne, was "the last member of the Moody family." She died in Racine, July 14, 1925, at the age of eighty-four. Singularly did she resemble her famous brother! The same vitality--she taught a Sunday school class in the First Presbyterian Church of Racine until the year of her death. She held toward D. L. the hero worship of a younger sister. She gathered and retained "every precious fragment," making numerous notations on sheets of paper, the backs of old photographs, etc., that have the highest historical value.[3]

In Elizabeth Moody Washburne's collection are values too numerous for complete inventory: scores of hitherto unpublished pictures; D. L.'s own letters running from boyhood days in Boston to sundown in Northfield; many of the letters of his mother, Betsey; and of his wife, Emma Charlotte Moody; most of the very mortgages, releases, deeds that in themselves could tell the pitiful struggle of the widow of Northfield; her last will and testament; the Masonic apron and contract for deed to pew number thirteen, belonging to D. L.'s father; D. L.'s army pass; bits of linen woven by Betsey's own hand, and articles of furniture belonging to her-pewter cups, Colonial chairs, china, spinet desk.

But the two jewels in this trust are: the little book, *Hymns and Prayers,* from which Betsey read to her bereaved family; and her Bible, the famous Mother's Bible in which she entered in her own hand the record of her family of nine; and in which she filed clippings of poetry, household remedies and spiritual comment. We exhibited some of these relics Sunday night, July 26, 1935, to hundreds of people in Moody Memorial Church.

*   *   *

I cannot forbear a brief account of the most dramatic experience in the search for biographical

[3]Permit a brief notation upon this Washburne family. Doctor and Mrs. Washburne had several children, including Miss Miriam. One was Franklin Bryant, Junior, who lives in Florida. He has a son, Franklin Bryant Washburne, who-lives in Hollywood! And I am indebted to the latter, whom many will remember in "Rupert of Hentzau," for valuable help.

data. The Fleet Chariot, which bore Deborah and myself, racing southward out of Quebec, descended the Atlantic slopes of the Maine mountains, pressed on through Augusta, Portland, "down to Dover," and finally into Keene, New Hampshire. We were at last in the borders of the Moody country, through the coveted Canadian approach. A few miles more and we would come to Northfield, Massachusetts. If only we could make it before dark! Late afternoon, June glory was upon the tumbling Ashuelot River as we flew along its bordering concrete ribbon. Hinsdale; a left turn south; into the Connecticut Valley, and, in seven miles, the gates of Northfield Seminary.

Swiftly we turned in, as twilight settled down; parked the auto, and climbed the gentle slopes of Round Top. Our eyes looked out over the very country, where in a true sense, Dwight Lyman Moody lived and moved and had his being. Within a few steps below the little hilltop was the house in which he was born; and almost adjoining, to the west, the homestead where he lived the last quarter of a century of his life. Southward in the soft evening lights lay Northfield with its long tree-lined main street; westward, the crest line of the Berkshires; eastward, the apparently continuous ridge of the Holyokes. And it seemed fitting, indeed, that on the little crown of Round Top, beneath the shadow of the trees, were two simple headstones, "companions in rest." One bore the name, "Dwight Lyman Moody, 1837-1899"; the other, "Emma C. Revell, wife of Dwight Lyman Moody, 1843-1903." Lo, we shall never be ashamed to admit that a tearful silence of prayer fell upon us.

From that time to this, my heart has lingered on Round Top, looking out upon the whole of Pilgrim's life from its gentle eminence. Though my little study is Beside the Golden Gate, yet in a mystic sense, I shall write upon Round Top.

*   *   *

As I inscribe the foreword, many months of research are ended, and the real task starts. The candles of Christmas are beginning to shed their soft glow over the world. Thanks be unto Him who enabled us to go scouting! I rejoice to find in my heart a writer's urge, a curious warmth which I fancied had passed away forever when *The Shadow of the Broad Brim* was completed. There is a sweet assurance that, if He will provide guidance in the writing of subsequent chapters, this book will serve to prove that God's chosen instrument is "My human best, filled with the Holy Spirit"; that today's broken world, to quote D. L. himself, needs nothing more than

Men and women on fire with the Fire of heaven; not great men, but true honest persons God can use.

R. E. D.

San Francisco,
December 5, 1935.

I
KING ARTHUR'S YEOMEN IN THE CONNECTICUT VALLEY

(From the Great Removal of 1635 to the marriage of
Edwin and Betsey Moody, 1828)

I have a most cheerful hope that the narrative I am now to write will, under the divine blessing, be a means of spreading what of all things in the world every benevolent heart will most desire to spread, a warm and lively sense of religion. Nor do I fear to tell the world that it is the design of my writing these memoirs, to spread this glorious and blessed enthusiasm, which I know to be the anticipation of heaven, as well as the most certain way to it.–*Phillip Doddridge, "Life of Col. James Gardiner."*

King Arthur's Yeomen in the Connecticut Valley
(1635-1828)

It is a rewarding approach, in viewing the life of the Commoner of Northfield, to stand upon Round Top, as it were, look out over the Connecticut Valley, and envision the six generations of Puritan ancestors from whom, through both father and mother, "he derived his pedigree." Let imagination pass in review those Broad Brimmers who for over two hundred years before Moody was born pioneered along the Connecticut River, figured prominently in every important enterprise, and were among those who laid the foundations of Northfield itself.

Aye, carry back thy ken *more than three hundred years from 1937*, and see D. L.'s ancestors, John Moody and William Houlton, arriving in America within twelve months of each other. Then trace their two family lines until, on January 3, 1828, they were bound together in the marriage of Edwin Moody and Betsey Holton. And it is well, also, to remember that Edwin and Betsey conveyed to D. L. what they had also received, blood relationships to other Puritan lines—the Edwards, Shattuck, Cox, Deming, Kellog, Alexander families. Let us trace these two tribes of Puritan forebears.

*　　*　　*

In 1633, Moody's paternal great-great-grand-father's great-grandfather, John Moody, of Bury,

17

St. Edmunds, England, arrived in "Roxbury" (ancient Boston suburb) in the fortieth year of his age. Behind him lay a fairly picturesque ancestry. His own great-grandfather Edmund was knighted in 1540 for saving the life of Henry VIII. . . With John Moody came Sara Cox, his wife, in the thirty-seventh year of her life. They were a childless couple. Four times in England she bore a child unto John, and each time they wept over a tiny coffin.

But the gift of God was soon to come to them again--and for the last time. Hooker and Stone, pioneer American real-estate boomers, promoted "a fertile section up the Connecticut River" with such California technique that in 1635 came "the Great Removal." Sixty men, women, and children left the Bay colony, going toward the Connecticut Valley with their cows, horses, and swine, bound for Hartford, "where they arrived after a tedious and difficult journey." And among the adventurers of the Great Removal were John and Sara Moody-- "she being great with child!" In Sara and John's pioneer Hartford cabin, 1636, was born Samuel, who grew up in the village and married Sarah Deming in 1658, both being twenty-two. The "pull of the upper valley" drew Samuel and Sarah, in 1660, to Hadley, Massachusetts, thirty-three miles north.

Now Samuel and Sarah begat six children, three girls and three boys, one of whom was Ebenezer, 1675.

And Ebenezer and Editha Owen begat nine children, four girls and five boys, one of whom was Joseph, 1720.

And Joseph and Sara Kellog begat eight children, two girls and six boys, one of whom was Noah, 1742.

And Noah and Susannah begat ten children, five girls and five boys, one of whom was "Isaiah of Northfield(!)" 1773.

And Isaiah and Phila Alexander begat nine children, four girls and five boys, one of whom was Edwin, 1800, father of Dwight Lyman Moody.

* * *

In 1634, one year after John Moody put out from Liverpool, the good ship *Francis* sailed for the New World. In her passenger list was a young chap, in his twenty-second year, William Houlton, of Suffolk, Ipswich. Undoubtedly he was a somebody, right down to the finer way in which he wore his buckles. Was he not an original proprietor of Mark Twain's town, and later of Northampton? And didn't he turn out to be a sort of pioneer Massachusetts congressman, in that he was for five years a representative on the General Court? So far as the church was concerned, behold, he was "Deacon Houlton, a goodly man!" It makes a fine picture to see him, as a member of the Second Settlement Committee, strutting like a senator, amidst the burned ruins of Squakeag (Northfield), pointing out where the new lines should run.

In 1640, William set up his home with Mary, a Puritan lass as blue-blooded as himself. And she begat eight children, five girls and three boys, one of whom was John, 1652.

And John and Abigail Day begat six children, two girls and four boys, one of whom was William, "a weaver," 1679.

And William and Abigail Edwards begat five children, two girls and three boys, one of whom was William (II) 1709, "who laid out Northfield by appointment of the General Court."

And William (II) and Azubah begat eight children, six girls and two boys, one of whom was Lemuel, 1749, "a very worthy and valuable man."

And Lemuel and Lydia Shattuck begat six children, one girl and five boys, one of whom was Luther "Holton," 1777 (note change of spelling).

And Luther and Betsey Hodges begat thirteen (!) children, nine boys and four girls, one of whom was Betsey Holton, February 5, 1805, mother of Dwight Lyman Moody.

*   *   *

It seems a pity that I must leave these family trees, worked out in full detail, after hours of painstaking research in New England. But the norms of modern biography, keyed to a high-speed psychology, demand that "two hundred feet of the film be cut right here."

These bare outlines, however, show the Moody and Holton families in the northern emigrations up the Connecticut Valley—two centuries of Indian perils, slow-moving herds and creaking, ox-drawn two-wheelers.

The two families "tied in" the first time on October 16, 1825, when Simeon P. Moody, cousin of

Edwin, was married to Fanny, one of "the four lovely Holton girls" who lived on the English grant right north of where Mount Hermon School is located.[1] Edwin Moody became interested in Fanny's younger sister, Betsey. Their ferry-boat courtship ended in marriage, January 3, 1828.

One has a better understanding of the relentless energy of Dwight Lyman Moody-his courage, his bluntness, his lack of poetic fancy, his sterling honesty-when he envisions the two hundred years of plain, home-loving, hard-working, upright "New England Vinegar Faces." One gets a clearer view of that shrewd, frugal, homely, hard-bitten thing called "Yankee"-the hybrid arising from Charnock's exacting Puritan theology crossed with the even more exacting conditions of a savage new world.

[1]See Fanny's picture, in group of four sisters, page 32.

THE GRANDMOTHERS

Betsey Hodges
Born 1781, died 1845
Married Luther Holton, 1801

(Photographed from oil-painting
in Holton Homestead,
Northfield, through courtesy of
Mrs. Minnie Holton Callendar)

Phila Alexander
Born 1781, died 1869
Married Isaiah Moody, 1799

(Washburne Collection)

II
SQUAKEAG CHANGES ITS NAME
(Northfield, from Gookin's visit, 1669, to the
Commoner's Centennial, 1937)

The history of Northfield, Franklin County, Massachusetts, is a rewarding study. No wonder Temple and Sheldon felt it was much worth while to understand "how civilized life was set up here, and how it finally displaced savage life." But it was her First Son, D. L. M., like the Mayos of Rochester, who set this Yankee village on such a hill that it could not be hid. The last census of American cities still ignores this New England Bethlehem; it is too little to be counted among the thousands of Judah. Yet out of it came a Willing Amasiah, who so greatly magnified his Ruler in Israel that thousands have followed thither to worship Him.—*Sketch Book.*

SQUAKEAG CHANGES ITS NAME
(1669-1937)

Four young Puritan surveyors rode horseback down Miller's River toward the Connecticut Valley, on a spring morning in 1669,-Captains Daniel Gookin, Thomas Prentice, Richard Beers, and Private Daniel Henchman. Making short work of a General Court Commission to lay out the new plantation which eventually became Worcester, they had two weeks to spare. Why not see what lay beyond in the northern wilderness? Why not?

When they reached the Connecticut River, they turned north and followed its tumbling course. It was the first time white man's eyes had looked upon the place. Decidedly it was "Indian Country." Blackened forest trunks rose up everywhere, the wreckage of the annual, fall fires, set to keep the country open for hunters. Only swamps and ravines had escaped the holocausts. Bluffs along the river, having adjacent brooks, were occupied by villages of shabby, smoking wigwams. Captain Gookin said, "This land lieth not in its primeval condition. The whole face showeth marks of savage occupancy, not improvement but devastation."

After cautious riding through the morning, they came to a part of the valley that "verily looked as heaven to us." What was its name? "Squakeag," grunted the Red Men. At least, that's how it sounded. Captain Gookin spelled it "Suckquakeag," and explained it meant "a place where one speared salmon." He also explained that "Connecticut" meant, "Quinneh" long (river), "tuk" (with waves). Not bad for this attractive four-hundred-mile stream rising in New Hampshire highlands and ending at the Atlantic, a bit east of the Yale Bowl! The land-hungry Puritans wanted Squakeag with all their hearts. Would the Indians sell it? Maybe, maybe! Captain Gookin's report to the governor had a postscript on it to the effect that a certain meadow land named "Suckquakeag" was a fair site for a village. And thus, the earliest beginnings of Northfield. The next year, 1670, acting on the report these four made to the governor, four other young men rode into Squakeag and found the Indians "eager to sell." Their eagerness arose from fear of a tribe of warlike neighbors; and they coveted protection from the white man's "smoking arrows."

In 1673, following the total purchases of 13,560 acres, sixteen families moved into this paradise of Northern Massachusetts. The exacting norms of biography again put a stop to the narrative, and I leave it with a sigh. But, there's gold in those quills for one who writes the story of the next thirty years: "the bold push of the Puritan pioneers," who snatched Squakeag from "its wide circle of wilderness."

The redemption of Squakeag was certainly not a perfumed amity. Three times it had to be colonized. The rude stockade and log huts built in 1673 were burned by gaggling savages in 1675. In wild fury

Richard Beers, one of the four who first saw Squakeag, rode to the defense, and a marker, somewhat weed grown, beside the Northfield Main Street shows the traditional spot where friends found his mutilated body.

Seven years later, 1682, pioneer zeal flared afresh. By 1684 the village streets were resurveyed, and in 1685 twenty families arrived. It was on the second settlement committee that we find the name of Moody's forebear, William Houlton (I). But the second settlement also, was short-lived. Red savages, instigated by the wily French Catholics of Quebec, stole down from the Canadian north. Peril quite up to the best western tradition settled down on the pioneers: "We came to a captive hung to a limb of a tree by a chain hooked in his jaw." So terrible did their onslaught become that a horseman rushed into Northfield, June 25, 1690, with this order from the County Court: "Get your corn and livestock to Springfield within six to eight days." Yelling savages, dancing in the lurid fires of burning buildings on the night of July 1, 1690, marked the failure of the second settlement.

For twenty years thereafter "the land lay with the savages." Then peace between warring mother countries in Europe abated for a time the duplicity of French Canadians. In the spring of 1714, caravans of two-wheelers and cattle moved back toward Squakeag. Around the night-fires beside the Connecticut arose the voices of men, women, and children singing the "O Suzannah" substitute of the Puritans:

The hosts of God encamp around
The dwellings of the just;
Protection He affords to all
Who make His name their trust!

But the General Court order upon which the men of 1714 colonized used the word "Northfield." Squakeag had changed its name! From now on "Northfield," because northernmost of Colonial settlements; a spear-head to be held against the Canadian approach for the next thirty-five years. In this third settlement appears the name of William Holton (II), Moody's great-great grandfather, as the "surveyor" who laid out the town upon General Court order.

The century following 1714 must, for our purpose, be swiftly sketched. While there was no longer danger of abandoning the village, yet during the first thirty-four years, to August 2, 1748, the villagers lived in constant peril of Indian snipers, influenced by merciless French Canadians. The period is replete with tragedies such as this, recorded in Pastor Doolittle's fascinating document:

Aug. 11, 1746. "A small party of Indians came to Northfield, shot upon Benjamin Wright a young man as he was riding after cows to bring them out of the woods; but his Horse brought him into town and he died the following night."[1]

From 1748 to 1800 came the period of peaceful occupation. The settlers profited by fading Indian

[1]Temple and Sheldon, *History of Northfield*.

traditions, learning from them how to make good old New England maple-sugar, and refraining from planting corn "until white oak-leaves grow big as squirrel paws." They erected their water-power trip-hammers, sythe factories, castor- and linseed-oil mills, rigging "water engines" for sash and blind factories. The social news of that day had a quaint flavor:

> "Seth Lyman (remember that name) who lives on the Second Brook has a daughter . . . so adept as to spin two threads at once, one with each hand, on the water-power spinning-wheel set up by her father."

The religious life was nominally Unitarian: but that word had none of the connotations of the present day.

The differences between the early New England Unitarian Churches and the Orthodox centered upon points of speculative theology. "Could God condemn a great part of the human race for His own good pleasure? Would a soul be lost because it was unwilling to be damned if God in His secret will so ordained?" No! said the Unitarian. Yes! thundered the Orthodox. Otherwise, Unitarian churches, in that early day, affirmed an inspired Bible and Jesus as the Saviour, with just enough of "a fatal angle of divergence" to finally put Ichabod over their church doors.

The first de facto pastor of the Northfield Church was Rev. Benjamin Doolittle,

"who died Jany Ye 9
1784 in the 54 year
of his age and 30th
year of his ministry"

The old, black head-marker in the cemetery with its dim inscription hints that he came to grief with his flock by being "well skilled in two important arts, both of preacher and physician," but that "Now he enjoys a sweet repose and when the just to life shall rise, Among the first he'll mount the skies."

The great awakening of 1733 powerfully moved upon Northfield. In fact, Jonathan Edwards himself held a revival in the little village, which "shook the mountains clear up to Canada." He deposited in the minds of Moody's forebears a heritage of sound thinking that eventually came to the boy as a part of the very atmosphere of the town. Something of the peculiar composure which faith gave these early heroes and heroines is sensed in the inscription upon the headstone, in the Northfield Cemetery, of a blood-relative of Moody's, Abigail Alexander, who died at the age of twenty-five:

"Friends and physicians could not save
This mortal body from the grave,
Nor can the grave contain it here
When Christ commands it to appear."

As nearly as we can estimate, William Holton (III) received from the King of England, in the year 1715, the grant of a parcel of land, a little south of Northfield, on the west side of the Connecticut and just north of Mount Hermon School. Here he strung his slate-fence posts—many of which are alive to this day—and here he began his quaint Yankee House-Barn (All hooked up together. Great in winter when one desires a basket of wood; but in summer, run for the fly-swatter!). And here the decidedly aristocratic Holtons struck root, flourishing with Rooseveltian families for two centuries. The property has continued in the Holton family on that ancient grant to this very year, 1936. One day in July, 1935, Mrs. Minnie Holton Callendar, "the last of the residentees," permitted me to carry the great oil-painting of her grandmother, Betsey Hodges, out into the sunlight to be photographed for reproduction in this book. There she is, Moody's maternal grandmother, looking for the world like a Puritan Mona Lisa!

In the summer of 1796 a devil-may-care chap, twenty-three years old, rode into Northfield from Hadley. Being a brick-mason, he was attracted by a report of much activity in his trade; and his whole fortune was "the horse he rode, and his kit of tools in a bag."[2] Here come the Moodys! for that brick-mason was Isaiah, grandfather of D. L.! Within three years, 1799, this vigorous knight of the trowel had wooed and won Phila, of the patrician Alexanders. Wasn't she of the blue-bloods who dated clear back to George Alexander, one of the four young fellows who rode up the Connecticut in 1670 and found the Indians eager to sell? And didn't she

[2] Temple and Sheldon, page 499.

have a mind of her own? And didn't Isaiah come to be known as *her husband?* And can't one make his own guess of all this from her picture? There she is, Moody's paternal grandmother, looking for the world like good Yankee Tenacity. Look at them both! *They* certainly had something to pass on to posterity! And we're quite sure D. L. got his share.

So we hang up a rough, early-day tapestry of the tiny but lovely village of Northfield. It never was large—415 in 1765; 1,641 in 1875; and 1,950 in 1936. But from the Holton Homestead appeared the Berkshire Madonna; and from the home of the itinerant brick-mason a son, Edwin. From the union of Edwin and Betsey, poignantly sweet in genuine love and deep distress, there was born in the fulness of time a humble post-Puritan lad, set to exhibit in a transforming measure the light of the knowledge of the glory of God in the face of Jesus Christ.

BERKSHIRE MADONNA
(Three pictures, from the Washburne Collection)

THE FOUR HOLTON SISTERS
Martha Holton Allen
Betsey Holton Moody
(At age of 65)
Fannie Holton Moody
Mary Holton Farrell

THE MOODY FAMILY, JULY, 1882
"First and only time they were together after Isaiah (first
from left in front row) ran away from home."
‑Elizabeth Moody Washburne
(fifth from left, top row)

(Key to this picture on following page)

Betsey Holton Moody
(At age of 84)

KEY TO FAMILY GROUP ON PRECEDING PAGE

(Seated, left to right): Isaiah, 1828-1916; Mother Moody, 1805-1896; George F., 1833-1905.

(Standing, left to right): Edwin, 1834-1907; Cornelia (Walker), 1830-1910; Samuel, 1841-1876; D. L., 1837-1899; Elizabeth Clapp (Washburne), 1841-1925; Luther, 1835-1890; Warren, 1841-1896.

III
BERKSHIRE MADONNA
(February 5, 1805–January 26, 1896)

"If I can control myself I would like to say a few words. It's a great honor to be the son of such a mother. I have traveled a good deal but I never saw one who had such tact. She so bound her children to her that it was a great calamity to have to leave home. The first year after my father died she wept herself to sleep every night. Yet she was always bright and cheerful in the presence of her children. Her sorrows drove her to Him. . . I would wake up and hear her praying, sometimes weeping. I cannot say half enough. That dear face! No sweeter on earth! Fifty years I was always glad to come home. When I got within fifty miles of home, I always grew restless and walked up and down the car. . . I was so glad I got back in time to be recognized. I said 'Mother, do you know me?' She said 'I *guess* I *do*.' I like that word, that Yankee word 'guess'! Here is her Bible; everything came from it! Widow Moody's light burned on that hill fifty four years. God bless you, mother; we love you still. Good-bye for a little while, mother!"
-D. L. at his mother's funeral-from Washburne Collection.

BERKSHIRE MADONNA
(1805-1896)

Betsey Holton Moody was born, 1805, on the same day of the month as her eminent son, February 5. His life was so profoundly shaped by his mother that her life is sketched in this separate chapter. After considerable inquiry in Northfield, we finally located the house in which she was born. It is the old Holton Homestead, mentioned in the previous chapter. The present generation of Northfielders seems to be losing that community cunning whereby a stranger is intrigued through a ready answer to his, What meaneth these stones? If the Homestead were in the land of All Year Boosters, the tires of hurrying motor-cars would be squealing day and night; squealing as tourists, upon the sight of a neon sign, "Birth Place of D. L. Moody's Mother," would come to a quick stop. Maybe it's better as it is.

If you want to visit this house as part of your centennial pilgrimage, you'll find it just opposite Mount Hermon School, on the north side of the Greenfield Highway. A few rods after one leaves the bridge over the Connecticut River and ascends the grade, there it is, in the delectable Berkshire Mountains. Don't forget those are the *Berkshire Mountains!* We were neatly warned by a budding geologist putting in a service-station summer not to call them "the Green Mountains as these locals do. It was the *Berkshire Range,* swinging southward on a wide sweep into North Adams and finally into New York State." For good measure this college lad added, "Those mountains over there (east side of Connecticut) are the Holyokes, not 'Northfields' as the locals say." Having raised the issue, we safely walk out with Pilate while the truth is being decided.

The old Homestead, some portions of which were begun by William Holton in 1715, proved a biographer's mother lode. There was, for instance, that twelve-by-fifteen-inch wall scroll, headed in a Spencerian hand, "Life How Short; Eternity How Long!" and subscribed by "Eldad White, January 15, 1829." The body of the little document had full answers about the thirteen children of D. L.'s grandparents, Luther and Betsey (Hodges) Holton, that even Temple and Sheldon omitted.

Here, in this Mellow Colonial, came the third child of Betsey Hodges and Luther Holton–Betsey, February 5, 1805. One can see a mile or so southward, from the room in which she was born, the impressive buildings of Mount Hermon School. It is substance for the tissue of dreams to think how a son of this country girl was literally to transform the landscape around the ancient Homestead.

Four of these thirteen children were girls. Their picture, reproduced here from the Washburne Collection, is a study of four women well filled with years; but their abiding grace, even in age, bears out every tradition as to the loveliness of their girlhood. The old spinning-wheel in the parlor (*still there*) tells something of Betsey's youth, when young ladies were trained in "the polite arts." An early writer described her as "a skillful spinner and weaver, able to copy all neighborhood patterns, and make some of her own." Deborah has from the Washburne Collection a precious square of finest linen woven by Betsey. What a mercy of God, that solid home training, when one recalls the widow of Northfield with nine to clothe and feed!

Very early records lift up four interesting facts: her father Luther believed in old-time evangelism: she had bright and merry ways: her training in the little red schoolhouse entirely ceased in her thirteenth year: and for the next ten years she was occupied in the practical duties of a home "where there was always a baby." "Such a background assured habits of industry, self-sacrifice and economy." In her twenty-first year came Edwin Moody, his ferry-boat courtship, and their marriage in her twenty-third year.

Put together the scattered bits that the past offers concerning her young husband. In form and size, his celebrated son resembled him; but here the likeness almost ceases. Edwin was a free-handed, careless, popular, lovable fellow: a brick-mason as was his father. It is cautiously admitted that "he tippled–slightly"! The Washburne Collection has in it Edwin's Masonic apron and vellum certificate, showing his admission to the Third Degree in the Harmony Lodge of Northfield, March 22, 1826. This sheepskin has on it one of his three or four extant signatures. Another document is a contract for a deed to pew thirteen in the Northfield Church, to be conveyed "to Edwin Moody, Bricklayer, for $131.00, payable $11.79 annually." Instalments are marked paid for about five years only. And another document underwrites insurance in the sum of $700.00 to Edwin Moody, *Yeoman.*

After their marriage, Edwin and Betsey moved into the honeymoon-house built by Cousin Simeon Moody, just at the northern edge of Northfield. This building is another example of "a New England process house." Today, it is brave in white paint, and a dignified plate announces it as "The Birthplace" to the thousands of pilgrims traveling with the decades. But when Edwin bought the place, in 1828, the house sat unpainted in a treeless pastureland at the base of a little bald knob (Round Top). Its water supply came down in an aqueduct from the mountains. A road passed in front, choking-dusty from sheep hoofs in the summer, and a sea of mud in the spring when the thaws began.

Two days each year Edwin journeyed to Boston over the stage-coach country, to trade his farm crops and Betsey's loom work. Remember, the railroads had not yet entered. The first train of the Central Vermont, with its pioneer New England equipment, did not puff into Northfield until April 15, 1849.[1]

On the first Boston trip after marriage he saw a newly printed Bible. Never mind the high price; he wanted it for *her!* And she, receiving it as a

[1]Letter from R. G. Gardner, Chief Engineer, Central Vermont, January 18, 1936.

fragrant gift of love, wrote into the family pages the records of her loved ones. That Bible is the jewel of the Washburne Collection. Edwin's improvidence came to a climax in a foolish gesture of friendship whereby stifling indebtedness fell upon the homestead. All the papers of filing and the pitiful redemptions worked out in later years by the widow are in the Collection; as are also the pictures of the hard-bitten mugs of Mr. and Mrs. Scrooge, who held the mortgages!

Let no man, however, fancy that this marriage was aught than one of abiding love. Despite poor Edwin's basic weaknesses, Betsey's heart never lost its love-song for him. There is that pathetic little loop of black hair in the Collection, of which Miss Miriam Washburne writes: "When Betsey's seventh child, Warren, was born, she felt so miserable she feared for her life. So she clipped a tiny piece from her raven tresses and braided it for Edwin to wear near his heart, after she. . ."

But it was to turn out far otherwise. Three years later, May 28, 1841, Edwin, laying stone, was seized with a pain from overexertion . . ."went home . . . staggered to the bed, knelt in a posture of prayer, and death took him before we really knew he was seriously ill." One month *later*, June 24, the twins, Elizabeth and Samuel, were born. Elizabeth subsequently wrote a tiny notation, which I found in the Collection, "I never remember mother's hair any other way than white; it turned quickly and completely after father died."

Canadian winter never roared down on Northfield

with greater bitterness than did the disaster of Edwin's death upon the home of the widow, with the seven children, and two tiny babes. In the long summer that followed the burden became almost intolerable to her. The neighbors said, "Give up some of your children, at least." One night after the children were asleep, she prayed, wept softly, then picked up the Bible Edwin had given her. For a long time she wept over it with bowed head. Then she dried her eyes and "opened it at random."

Who can doubt but that angelic hands directed her eyes to see Jeremiah 49:11: "Leave thy fatherless children, I will preserve them alive; and let thy widows trust in me." The old Bible today shows around the passage the trembling pencil marks of the young widow. It was as if Edwin held counsel with her. "Oh, God," she sobbed, "I *know* that thou hast given these children to me and that thou wilt be a Father to them if I will do a mother's part." Here we find the bidings of her power; as C. I. Scofield said, "Thus, in the circle of these hills, God brought our sister to this greatness."

There is no need for a detailed account of the pathetic years of struggle following, or of the widow's heroism, when sometimes she even worked out in Northfield homes. We submit as a sample of the trying years the crisis of 1854. At that time Mr. and Mrs. Scrooge, who held Edwin's mortgage notes, foreclosed upon "all moveables and took even the wood in the shed." The dear little old gentlewoman of the Holton Homestead, Mrs. Callendar, will tell you, if you desire, the beautiful story of how her father Cyrus, Betsey's brother, promptly delivered to the beleaguered widow what D. L. thought was "the largest load of wood he ever saw in his life."

But the stricken home fashioned quickly into a university of the highest order. Betsey regimented poverty like a general. Through grace abounding she kept her fatherless group together; sent them to school; by her loom magic caused them to appear on the Lord's day in Pastor Oliver Capen Everett's church decently clothed, and therefore in their right minds. (Sound psychology in that ancient Scripture!) If quarrels came in the home, "I prayed, and when I came back, they would all be good children again."

There was another very dark passage when Isaiah, reckless son with a scarred face, ran away to sea, June 2, 1844, vanishing for twelve weary years. But Betsey kept the mother's light burning; hoping, praying. On winter nights, she sat with her eight children about the fireplace. She repeated to them the endearing twice-told tales about the dead father: how he looked; how she loved him; how he was good to everybody; how he was kind to a friend and thereby the home was mortgaged. D. L. remembered in after years that if one of them chanced to speak of missing brother she always sobbed, "while we whispered 'good night' and stole away to bed." And he had no more touching proof of Christ's love for sinners than in telling how Isaiah, returning home years later, was forgiven by his mother "before he asked for it."

The religion of Betsey's youth and early widowhood was nominally Unitarian. The content of her early belief seems chiefly to have been a simple trust in God, and a deep loyalty for Puritan ethics. When the tempests broke over her home, she called unto Him out of the depths, and walked with Him by faith. She had deep devotional instincts, "reading to her children summer evenings under the great sugar maples, from the little book[2] of sacred poetry!" But in her early widowhood she knew very little of those great Christian doctrines of faith upon which Puritan homes majored: no one had ever taught her, and in consequence, she, having need to learn, could not teach them to her children. Of this D. L. once spoke with pathos to Spurgeon: "You have the advantage of hearing these matters from your youth up, while I must laboriously seek them out." Her pastor, O. C. Everett, however, deserves high recognition. He began his work in the Northfield Unitarian Church as a very young man, a few weeks after Moody was born, and served until "he was dismissed, November 26, 1848." This faithful shepherd might well have been the study for Barrie's *Little Minister*. Precious was his care for the widow and her bairns.

*   *   *

But, when one of her *own* bairns decided to become a preacher, she disapproved. In fact she "would never consent to hear Moody preach until

[2]"From this book my mother used to read morning and night with her family of nine children gathered about her." (Note by Elizabeth Moody copied from the little volume.)

after he came to renown."[3] The very first time she ever listened to him was in the Northfield Congregational Church, August, 1876. D. L. was now world famous. The family, just about to drive down to the church was startled to hear her say, "I don't suppose there would be room for me in the wagon this morning?"[4]

D. L. was surprised and deeply moved upon seeing his mother in the congregation. When those who wished prayer were asked to stand up, she arose with others. B. F. Jacobs said, "Moody was overcome. He turned to me and said, 'You pray, Jacobs, I can't.'" The inner story of her spiritual history, almost buried in yesterday's documents, shows that she had been led little by little into the deep things of the Word. Increasingly she sensed the low ceilings in her ancestral church. Her raised hand, bringing a rush of tears to D. L., was the evidence of her final decision to come into the full liberty of the gospel, and a mother's deep joy in her son. Farwell said, "She then became a member of the Congregational Church." But, it does not appear reasonable that she was *converted* at that time!

* * *

As age came upon her, she like her son, grew heavenward; "rising in spiritual power to a place among the historic mothers, the mothers of the Wesleys and of Augustine." Her letters in the Washburne Collection are documents of the Victorious

[3]Ed Kimball quoted in the *Chicago Tribune*, 1900.
[4]John Farwell, *Early Recollections of D. L. Moody.*

Life. Here is a quotation from one written in beautiful script, at eighty-six;

> "I do all my housework, except combing my hair. I have made butter all the winter and fall. You need not scold. I sometimes get pretty tired, but I soon get rested! *The good Lord gives me strength from day to day!*"

Other fragments show that she became a wide and careful reader of world events. There are many sheets of paper with outlines of texts which prove that she did very fair exegesis herself. Moody's love for her deepened to adoration. No wonder! He saw plainly that his great fame never pleased her half as much as the integrity of his life. More and more, notable Christians of the world were held in amazement by her Christian character; a charm exerted equally over the boys and girls of the Northfield Schools.

In 1889, Moody built for her the famous Octagon Room on the northwest side of the birthplace. There she could look out upon a magnificent view of the Connecticut River, and the northern mountains she loved so well.

Then came a day just before Christmas, 1895. The mysterious sense of death was upon her. Well, it was all right. Wasn't her work through? And hadn't God blessed her in all things in those ninety years? She wrote in a clear hand some closing lines of a last letter: "I often think how good the Lord has been to me all through my journey in this life. . . He has given me such good children. . ."

She stopped to wipe a tear from her aged eyes. Yes, God *had* been good to her. Out from the window of her west-facing room lay a wide-spread panorama of snow-bound New England glory; something like that far-off day when little Dwight cried beside her. On the horizon line to the north stood Brattleboro Mountain, purple and patched with white. There were the forests upon which she had looked ever since Edwin brought her there sixty-eight years ago. The last rays of setting sun glared up like molten bronze from the icy curves of the river. Out from her papers she drew the little love knot. . . Dear God how many were the years since she prepared it for Edwin! The aged lips moved—even sensible people sometimes speak to their beloved dead—"Oh, Edwin, if you only knew, how glad you'd be to see the children our God hath given us!"

*　　*　　*

On Friday, January 24, 1896, she took to her bed. D. L. hastened back from a great meeting for the precious closing moments. He dropped beside her bed and sobbed, "Mother! Mother! do you know me?" And her calm voice replied, "Well, I *guess* I *do!*"

On Sunday morning, January 26, she "made the good entrance". . . It was poetic justice that her simple casket was escorted to the Northfield Church by four hundred young women from the Seminary, and a column of young men from Mount Hermon.

Her grave lies in a fenced-off section of the ancient cemetery down by the Vermont Central depot; right on the edge of a little, tree-clad bluff dropping down to the Great Meadow of the Connecticut. Edwin lies beside her, his stone bearing that precious text from Jeremiah 49:11, which seemed to her in the first lonely days of widowhood to be both his voice and God's. And on her own, the simple grandeur of Mark 14:8, "She hath done what she could."

It moved us unto "tender thanksgiving," upon looking across the Connecticut River from her graveside, to behold the Berkshire Mountains, where she was born. And in plain sight, as if in testimony to her Christian motherhood, the castled beauty of Mount Hermon School.

THE BIRTHPLACE
(Washburne Collection)

    With the exception of the young maples, the above picture shows the birthplace as it looked when D. L. was born, 1837. This drawing was made by Elizabeth Moody Washburne, about 1852, she being then 12. The house was originally built by Simeon Moody, 1823; purchased by Edwin (D. L.'s father), 1828; title now held by the trustees of the Northfield Schools. It is a shrine of American evangelical faith. For a view as it is today, see page 322.

IV
PRESUMPTION HEADS UP TOWARD THE CITY OF DESTRUCTION
(February 5, 1837, to February 5, 1854)

The village interval of Moody's boyhood, though brief, was sufficient to give him a heart storage from which he was, to the end of his days, bringing forth treasures. There were the haunting glories of the Northfield heath; there were the homely and vital experiences of farm life, that became little vignettes for ruggedly setting forth eternal truth. But the chief good was the abiding power of the widowed mother's sterling character, and the crystal purity of his love for her. Pictures filled his memory: he could see her at the old spinning-wheel, or absorbed in the Mother's Bible; or he could hear her night-sobbed prayers as Nor'easters moaned over Round Top. These memories were employed by a Divine One to soften him like fire, and they ended by making precious to him every one of her own ethical ideals. So it is always with a Good Mother! Though he rose to such giant stature that he was described as putting one hand on England, one on America and moving both nations toward the Throne, yet in his heart he was always *her boy*, esteeming it a privilege angels might covet to soften the asperities of her early days with heaped up comforts for her latter.- *Sketch Book.*

Presumption Heads Up Toward the City of Destruction
(1837-1854)

"Dwight L. Ryther Moody was born
Feb. 5th 1837.   Sunday"

Thus Betsey Holton Moody recorded in the Mother's Bible the birth of her sixth child. Fragments in the Washburne Collection explain why the name "Dwight L." (Lyman), was chosen. A mortgage clearance of 1850 describes the Lyman place as lying east and adjacent to the Moody farm; a stray sentence refers to "Dwight Lyman's having been kind to Betsey." Behind all this lay an interfamily friendship dating back to the Great Removal. And the explanation is completed when one reads an incision upon a leaning slate, in the old cemetery down by the depot:

"Josiah Dwight Lyman.   Born Feb. 27, 1780.
Died Jan. 5, 1869   Ae 88"

But "Ryther," the portion quickly discarded and practically unknown today, here was a *quod libet* that came out like a slow negative. But, it came out! And it makes a good story. Lt. David Ryther, a stout, old, British army man, came to America on the square-rigger *Lion*, and met there a young friend whom he knew first in England, Isaiah Moody. They became fellow émigrés in Hooker and Stone's

49

"Great Removal to Hartford," 1636. Lt. Ryther married Martha Shattuck, who bore him eleven children, five girls and six boys, several of whom settled in Bernardston. That's the village a few miles southwest of Northfield where, in going to Greenfield, one turns left at the traffic beacon. ("You *cahn't* miss it," they tell you when you ask directions. And by the way, if you ever tour New England, you'll hear in your dreams, "Bear right; or left; traffic beacon; you *cahn't* miss it!" And then you *do* miss it!)

Dr. Gideon Ryther was a Bernardston descendant. Edwin Moody (D. L.'s father) did stonework for him. Now these fruitful and multiplying New Englanders, "hard pressed for handles," often named their babies after neighbors; and the neighbors, thus honored, usually "came through with a lamb for the baby." So if Doctor Ryther overlooked a pleasant tradition, could the Moodys be reproached for dropping "Ryther"?

*   *   *

Deborah and I set ourselves to see, as thoroughly as we could, the world in which Dwight Lyman Moody spent his boyhood. To this end we entered and retraveled Massachusetts by the Canadian approaches. Well worth while it was to behold the Connecticut River, before it runs softly at Northfield, go hurrying through narrow cañons whose tali were dusky with balsam, pine, and spruce. We drew infinitely closer to Moody as we became familiar with the haunting beauty of New England—

a memory-wall picture whose composition is dark-forested mountain sides, rolling hills and sunny meadows, where, scattered like gems, are the sweet sincerities of Colonial houses. One just can't help dreaming when he gazes upon those comely vales through which successively passed fire-careless Red Men, buckled Puritans, red-coated Britishers, and stolid Yankee farmers. And today those same sylvan beauties are possessed by a new race, moving in flashing chariots on ribbon-smooth highways, highways that run ever and anon beside blue waters, smart with white sails and snapping with the machine-gun rattle of aquaplanes. New England! No wonder he loved it! And we'll fervently say for ourselves, "You *cahn't* miss it!"

When Moody was a boy, many relics of Indian occupation remained: old mounds, underground granaries, and stone ax-heads, which an active lad could find. But the natural world was widely different from the wreckage the pioneers beheld. The eyes of young Moody looked upon companies of young trees hopefully moving into the meadows, and upon the hillsides, clouds of rock maple, soft maple, walnut, butternut, hickory-nut, with ever and anon the coral beauty of blooming laurel. One can't help loving Northfield, all the way from the Great Meadow, lying along the Connecticut, "the village's ancient granary and storehouse," to the circling mountains.

Lift up your eyes to these mountains! Westward in the Berkshires are the crowns of Pisgah, Grass Hill and Pond Mountain (at whose base is the wide

White Lily Pond); eastward, in the seemingly continuous range line of the Holyokes, are the finger tips of Little Hemlock, Grace, Stonebridge, Stratton and Brush Mountains. "Surely," said Deborah as we cruised for hours along forgotten wagon roads, "this was a boy's world!"

Yea, verily and it was, all the way from the company of streams that come laughing down toward the Connecticut to the flowers and birds of the field. We quitted the inns, and deliberately slept out, just to be near the places and objects he loved. There were the west side brooks—Broad, Cold, and Bennetts; and on the east—Saw Mill, Cranberry, and Pauchaug. And there were his feathered friends: cat-birds with gossipy miauws; bobolinks wearing creamy epauletts; jay-birds; swallows; and fussy chickadees, upside down, eating their seed luncheons. And the flowers—columbine, wake-robin, dark violets on trinity leaves! "Lo!" said Deborah, "it is a boy's world!"

No wonder Northfield became to Moody the Land of Heart's Desire; and no wonder he returned from every wide apostolate to the glad serenity of his boyhood scenes! Here's a letter dated London, May 13, 1884:

> "My dear Ed Your buteful Pht of Nelley Gray and colt was handed me yesterday & it is just splendid She looks proud of her colt I am just longing to get home as Spring comes on I get homesick . . . Write me another good farme letter"

It was all to him as the well by the gate, whether it was the season when the Connecticut flowed in the leafy month of June, or winter, with its frosty breath, sleigh-bells, and leafless rock maples standing deep in the snow. To really *see* Northfield brings a sense of mystic fellowship with Moody as does no other experience.

* * *

But the loom patterns of this chapter have no tracings for the twice-told tales of his boyhood—captious lecture announcements, rail-fence dramas, ferry-boat prayers, cats-in-coffins, or squirrels-in-lunch-pails. Our interest hangs on how a headstrong boy, gifted to be sure with certain homespun graces, came nearly falling short, and certainly would have but for the young King who overtook him. The greatest centennial profit will reach us by observing how a compactly built, vigorous young Berkshire rustic became headstrong, reckless, malcontent; first in skip-jack pranks, and last in conscientious labor; and then to see how by Effectual Grace he came to himself. "When I was a boy, I hoed corn so poorly, that when I left off I had to take a stick and mark the place so I could tell next morning where I had stopped the night before." The Northfield pastor, Mr. Everett, saw the boy's perilous bias with a heavy heart. Once, to help if he could, he took D. L. into his own home "to do errands and go to school." But it didn't last long. "The dominie's patience was sorely tried."

It is not necessary to overlook the lad's simple

excellencies, the fine devotion toward his mother and his kinsfolk, the unquestioned moral fineness that marked him. In the little book "Hymns and Prayers for Children" (Washburne Collection), Elizabeth's handwriting on the fly-leaf informs us, "The verses marked were taught me when three years old by my brother D. L. M." (Then eight.) Nor can we dismiss as insignificant his shrewdness as observed in adolescent "swapping." There are some great institutions in this year, 1936, owing much to this Yankee cunning.

But, by the time our subject was sixteen he had become another Presumption, proudly considering himself "a good tub sitting on its own bottom." Actually, mournfully deficient! Ignorant! The ministry of the little red schoolhouse on the Squakeag was defeated so far as he was concerned. He went through about half a dozen terms, "but very little ever went through him!" Spiritually, dark! His training in spiritual truth was almost negligible. Here was a boy, soon to leave home, who "detested Sunday; I resented my mother compelling me after I had worked in the field all week to go to church and hear a sermon I couldn't understand." He had come to avoid books, slight his work, and excel in buffoon jokes.

In his sixteenth year spiritual misery became acute; nothing would do except getting away from Northfield. His first attempt was short-lived. The printing outfit down in Clinton couldn't tolerate his blunders in mailing addresses, and, to use a blunt term, "fired him." One blustery March afternoon, in 1853, he and Ed were cutting logs on Stonebridge Mountain. For some time his solid body had been rapidly bitting an ax against a tree bole, like Gideon with his flail. Suddenly he threw the ax down and blurted out, "*I'm sick and tired of this!* I'm not going to stay around here any longer. I'm going off to get some other work."

He didn't "get off" right away, however. Spring shifted into summer, into fall, and Thanksgiving Day of 1853 arrived. Samuel Socrates Holton and his brother Lemuel, "prominent shoe-dealers," came up from Boston to spend the day with their sister, Betsey Moody, and her family. Both brothers had helped Betsey financially during some of the bitter crisis-years after Edwin died. Samuel, now thirty-six, was accompanied by his second wife, Typhenia Clapp. Something about the miserable Dwight wakened in her a sympathy and affection that were later to have a large part in Moody's conversion. During the Thanksgiving dinner she couldn't keep her eyes off his flushed, downcast face.

She was not surprised, therefore, when D. L. suddenly said to her husband, "Uncle, I want to come to Boston, and have a place in your shoe-store. Will you take me?" Uncle Samuel looked across the table to Betsey, "Shall I take him?" Brother George, twenty-one, yelled, "No! he'll soon want to run your store!" D. L.'s brown eyes ran quickly around the circle. Amusement, consternation, or contempt were on all the faces save one. The glance of his young Aunt Typhenia revealed a sympathy that warmed his heart. He wouldn't forget it.

The fall of 1853 moved on in utter distaste to him. Rebellious at heart, he entered a peculiarly acute period of rowdy school conduct in January, 1854. Suddenly he was seized with remorse, and for the first time in his life began really to apply himself to his studies.

But it was too late! In a few days more home ties were to be broken and school days ended forever. For the rest of his life, our Jacob was to have a limp from shabby education. And his native rudeness, for so long time uncurbed and unchecked, fastened upon him and continued for many years, leaving behind, to his own deep grief, a trail of wounded feelings. George Pentecost was speaking of this trait, that, like his deficient education, struck its roots into his Presumptuous Years: "Poor old Moody: we all *love* him, but some of us don't *like* him."

On his seventeenth birthday, February 5, 1854 (according to an item in the Collection, apparently authentic), he permanently broke home ties, and started out for himself. And he was unmistakably headed toward the City of Destruction.

PRESUMPTION AT SEVENTEEN
(Washburne Collection)

(Notation on back of photo: "Taken by F. D. Hopkins, photographist (sic), 51 Washington St., near Hanover, Boston")

D. L. at age of 17

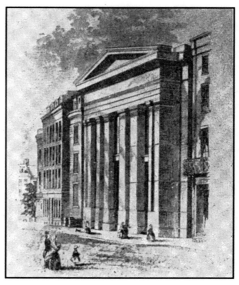

Mount Vernon Congregational Church, Boston

Where D. L. united after he was "overtaken" through Edward Kimball

V
BUT IS OVERTAKEN BY THE KING
(1854-1856)

"I can truly say, and in saying it I magnify the infinite grace of God as bestowed upon him, that I have seen few persons whose minds were spiritually darker than was his when he came into my Sunday school class; and I think the committee of the Mount Vernon Church seldom met an applicant for membership more unlikely ever to become a Christian of clear and decided views of gospel truth, still less to fill any extended sphere of public usefulness."–*Letter of Edward Kimball to Nason and Beale.*

BUT IS OVERTAKEN BY THE KING
(1854-1856)

When the odd little train of the Central Vermont stopped at Northfield that winter's morning of 1854, D. L., just seventeen, decked out in his best, was ready to climb aboard. "It seemed mighty good to a man" (so his adolescent letters affirm), to be striking off for himself. Of course he regretted his mother's objections. Brother Ed pressed a five-dollar bill into his hand. Well, Ed wasn't so hardhearted after all. Tearful farewells; the shrill little blast of the locomotive-whistle–and he was gone. A day's chugging over the landscape of Massachusetts' winter wonderland–then Boston.

*   *   *

Well, first off, he'd show his Uncle Samuel something! He'd drop into his shoe-store simply as a casual visitor who happened to know Samuel's sister in the country. A large boil on his neck gave his head a ludicrous forward tilt over the left shoulder; that didn't click so well in the act. From Uncle Samuel's he went; over to Uncle Lemuel's, where he "lived a fortinet" (his own spelling). He began the week vigorously "looking about for a situation"; he ended it sensing failure. The last two days he "had that awful feeling that no one wanted me. I have never had it since and never want it again."

Noting the boy's depression, Lemuel said, "Why not ask your Uncle Samuel for a place?" "He ought to ask me," said the lad. His pride was wilting. "But I'll go see." . . Samuel looked sharply at the embarrassed boy. Twenty years ago he himself had come to Boston at seventeen, and that twenty years had caused him to see many young fellows go to pieces through lack of discipline. D. L. therefore should know the forge, the hammer, and the file. Yes, he would give D. L. a place; but there were conditions. He must board where he was told, keep off the streets at night, avoid questionable places of amusement, and regularly attend the Mount Vernon Church. Would Dwight agree? Yes! A thousand times, *Yes!*

His first boarding-place was Deacon Levi Bowers, on Allen Street. Later, Uncle Samuel designated Mrs. David Beal's, 5 Eaton Street. (While here he had the "boy-in-cap" picture taken which graces this chapter.) From there he moved into quarters directly over the shoe-store at 43 Court Street, just a step from Faneuil Hall.

The edifice of Mount Vernon Church, "an excellent and exact Congregational body," was on an inside lot in downtown Boston (then 150,000), a building in very good Greek design. Dr. Edwin N. Kirk was pastor, "a magnificent chap, physically, mentally, spiritually: he preached plain, loving sermons, and won the boy's wholesome respect." Sixteen years after D. L. began attending the Mount Vernon Church, Doctor Kirk, "grown venerable," visited Samuel Holton, now in midlife, at his im-

pressive suburban residence in Winchester. With a catch
in his voice, the minister said: "I'm just back from
Chicago. There is that young Moody we thought did not
know enough to be in our church, exerting a greater
influence for Christ than any man in the West. I'm
ashamed of myself."

Before we proceed with the narrative of D. L.'s
conversion, it is worth while to observe a little of his
Boston life. On the whole, he turned out to be a pretty
good clerk; and it was a very interesting experience to live
with the large company of young men in the quarters over
the store. There is one letter in the Washburne
Collection, written on foolscap paper, that I have regarded
with more interest than any other relic, save the Mother's
Bible. It is written in ink; the first page with painful
effort, letters shaded; the last three pages break down into
a mad scrawl. Spelling and punctuation are carefully
retained:

BOSTON June 5 1854

DEAR MOTHER

(He begins by explaining why he hasn't written)
. . . so much goin on here for the last fortinet . . . I was
happy to here from home every weak, but you ned not
think that I am homesick . . . the time goes by lik a
whirl wind how do the things look have you had any
pears yet   Where I bord thare is over 50 now and lots
of them about my age   There never was so much
excitement in this city be for Friday in the world   The
city was hung in Black and thare was a coffen hung

out the cabbin of liberty I got up in the secont story
. . . They took him (a negro) out about $2^{1/2}$ & such
a groaning and hising you never herd I was all
burnt up with the son   The poleus (police) came
up to the store and told us to come down but we
was up so he could not reach us . . . The negro
looked around when they led him off . . . I am getin
prety ragged about this time but I shall not be so
hard up long but 50 Dlrs dont got but a little ways
in sporting a man I go to meating at Mount Vernon
Orthedx I dont know how it is spelt . . . Tell
William Alexander not to hire before he sees me
for if I don't get a place in Dearsfield I shall want
to go to wok for him (Evidently not sure of "his
place" with Uncle Samuel). . . If I send you some
shoes I dont spose thay will fit becaus Calvin (a
fellow clerk) sent home 3 times befor he could fit
his mother and then he did not fit hur(!)   Mother
now dont think I cant read your writing I en read it
a good deal better than you can mine I can read you
as well as print   (Rather! his mother's hand was
unusually fine; his own remained to the end, a
dreadful scrawl)   I have bin 5 minits wrighting this
and have not got half don but if you can read it you
can do better than I can   Dwight (Yea, verily and
anyone does well to read it.)

*   *   *

We now reach the subject in which this chapter
has chief interest, the story of Young Presumption's
Being Overtaken, which, as Edward Kimball as-

serted, "magnifies the infinite grace of God as bestowed upon him." Once again we must take into account Samuel's wife, Typhenia Clapp Holton. (Remember the Thanksgiving dinner?) A photograph in the Washburne Collection shows that the fine oval face of this young woman was unmistakably spiritual; framed in jet-black hair, center parted, closely brushed. She was the second of the Clapp sisters married by her husband Samuel (he married three, Elizabeth, Typhenia and Georgianna). In the winter of 1857, a few months after D. L. left for Chicago, she came to the Gates of Glory.

But she was one of the Young King's first servants in helping overtake the rebellious boy. Hers was a radiant faith, and to her the lad opened wide his confidence:

"I like the pastor; and Mr. Kimball; but these rich and pious folks at Mount Vernon *make me sick and tired.*" (Delightful to find this pet phrase of D. L.'s. He was "sick and tired" of something or other all his life.)

"Never mind, Dwight, the Church is the Bride of Christ."

"But the young folks are so lofty and proud. Is that Christianity?"

"Lad, *we* are to fight the fight of faith. Do you love the Church?"

"Well, I guess I do!"

"Then forget the rest!"

When the wounds of the Lord came upon Moody's heart, she knew that in him there was beginning an effectual work of Grace. He poured out his heart to her. So, she led him into the Interpreter's House. Later, after conversion, when the fire of testimony "got in his bones," and he grieved over his limping speech, Typhenia said to him:

"Do you love Christ?"

"Well, I *guess* I *do!*"

"Then don't worry, lad, over how you talk; just try to tell the people what He has done for your soul, *and He'll do the rest.*"

It's a joy to bring this rare young woman out of the shadows that the years have cast. She was to Moody just what Mary King was to Spurgeon.

*   *   *

When Moody, acting upon Uncle Samuel's conditions, entered the Mount Vernon Sunday school, Superintendent Palmer assigned him to a class of boys taught by Mr. Edward Kimball. Kimball subsequently became known as "the champion church debt raiser of the United States." Most of his life was spent in church work. Moody appeared desperately needy to Kimball. Not until after a full year did he begin to feel "the burden of the Lord" for the boy. On the morning of April 21, 1855, he went down to the Holton store determined to speak to D. L. about his soul. "I made a dash for it to have it over at once." D. L. was in the back of the building wrapping up shoes. He looked small enough, with his one hundred and thirty-five pounds, mass of black hair overdue at the barbershop, full lips, heavy eyebrows, and dreamful brown eyes; quick, vigorous motions like a Maricopa quail. Kimball put his hand on his shoulder and made, as he thought, "a weak appeal." Years later he said, "I never could remember just what I *did* say: something about Christ and His love; that was all." But the heart of the future prince of God lingered a thousand times on that sweet moment. "I can feel his hand yet!" Marvelous the way of the Spirit. The "limping words" of Kimball were blessed—and the angels in heaven rejoiced that morning. Shortly after Kimball left the store, noon bells began to ring in the spring world of Boston. D. L. walked the streets "as in a dream." A thousand times in future years he relived that strange ecstasy of one who has just become a new creature in Christ Jesus:

> "I went out of doors and I fell in love with the bright sun shining over the earth. I never loved the sun before. And when I heard the birds singing their sweet song on the Boston Common, I fell in love with the birds. I was in love with all creation."

We omit here the transcription of the church records of Mount Vernon, reflecting the official misgivings as to Moody's conversion, and the consequent full year of delay in granting him membership. Lo, do not nearly all the lives reproduce this in full, just as meticulous Joseph Cook originally made the copy? The high drama for which we have eyes is that of a lad "revised by the King" stopping in the office of Kimball a few weeks after his receipt into church-membership, tearfully to tell his spiritual benefactor "Good-bye!" He had a grievance of some sort and he wanted to get away from Boston. "I'm going West. Uncle Sam doesn't want me to, so the quicker I get out of his way, the better. I'm starting this morning!"

During the succeeding years, Moody's rising fame made Kimball often thank God that he had not been disobedient to the heavenly vision. Just suppose that he had *not* spoken to the Northfield boy on that morning in April!

DOWNTOWN CHICAGO, TIME OF MOODY'S ARRIVAL, SEPTEMBER, 1856
(Courtesy Chicago Historical Society)

The Old Court House and the Chamber of Commerce

The Chamber of Commerce, the building in full-view, center of picture, was formerly the First Baptist Church, where Moody met Emma Charlotte Revell, and where they were married. See first paragraph of Chapter VIII.

VI
WESTWARD, HO!
(September, 1856-February, 1860)

The swift-falling, haphazard strokes that shaped the New West are curiously typical of Moody in the period of the following fifteen years. He was born again; very true. But he had yet to learn how great is the distance separating between the new birth and the Anointing with Power. He had a zeal for service; but it was deficient in Integrating Wisdom. No one is to be condemned for being in Moody's first spiritual frame. But anyone who *remains* there is a subject of tears. Moody saw it clearly after November, 1871. He then, deeply humbled, understood that a realtor's high pressure activity had to be replaced by Softer Walking Something Better. At first it was all touch and go with him. "Numbers were everything; and if numbers sagged, he was blue." Christianity had to have RUSH in it; Faith was a thing to be opened very early in the morning with an office key, and closed with a letter for the late mail. But in 1871, a much chastened man looked on those furious years and said, "I wouldn't go back for anything."-*Sketch Book.*

WESTWARD, HO!
(September, 1856-February, 1860)

The morning of September 13, 1856, marked the beginning of one of those halcyon fall days of Ohio and Indiana. An odd little locomotive, gay with red paint, polished brass, and Falstaffian flue, snorted through compact timber-lands. Here and there appeared clearings enclosed by rail fences, split from priceless black walnut. And there were plenty of stumps to be grubbed. Everybody waved at the train. Why not? It had been in operation only four years, and its shrill little whistle said as plainly as anything, "Civilization's coming."

The little thirty-foot coaches swayed perilously on the thirty-pound rails as the engine roared along at thirty miles. It was a new day, a new world, and a new deal! (We started talking that way very early.) Most of the passengers were grimy and dog-weary. Whale-oil lamps and tin wash-basins and no soft Pullman berths made travel serious business.

But *that boy!* Didn't he ever get tired? Back and forth, back and forth, rear platform, crowded aisles! In heaven's name, it made everyone weary just to watch his tireless energies. The only ones who apparently approved at all were the two dear old Christian women who got on the same train with him in Boston. The boy felt that the world was moving west, and so was he! The long line of

Conestoga wagons was still to be seen from the small windows of the coach, heading toward the sunset, toward "Chicago!"

Ah, but that was a magic word! The mill-race of settlers running through the primitive land had put one hundred and fifty thousand residents into the Garden City ahead of the boy. He was surely glad to be another. No wonder Brother Luther liked the West and had written *such* letters about it. And besides, he, Dwight, was through with Boston, "fairly drove out of it: his path crossed and his hopes blasted."

Night had fallen when the little train rumbled into the Chicago station, over the long trestle on Lake Michigan. So this was Chicago! Well, it looked good even by gaslight. The streets were laid out straight and broad–"not cowtrails, like *some* cities."

In the next few weeks, the fast-stepping youngster decided there were more dwelling-houses than he ever saw, scattered over four times the space of Boston. There were dirty streets, plank sidewalks on five different levels in every block, and plenty of mud; Lake Michigan's level was almost as high as Wabash Avenue. Pretty good thing though; made it easy for fellows delivering drinking water in those odd barrels lashed on two-wheeled carts. (Don't laugh! They get it a little further out now, and bring it in glass bottles or cast-iron pipes.) But it was "healthy"; he quickly fattened up to one hundred and fifty (with a hundred to go).

The streets were alive with traffic–horse-cars,

single seaters with spanking horses; high-hatted young
gents accompanying young ladies in high-waisted black
skirts, bulky as circus tents. Hardly a gray head any place!
(Gray heads all stayed in Boston.) Droves of young men!
And in the Lake there were covies of sailing freighters and
pencil-stacked side-wheelers. But there were also droves of
desperate little ragamuffins living near drains "where rats
came out to die."

In a few days he had a job in Wiswall's boot-and-shoe
store down on Lake Street. The letters of introduction
"worked." His very bluff and hearty style, which first gave
Wiswall much misgiving, turned out a real asset. In the
next two years, rough customers liked him so well that
"We had a rule 'Turn them over to Moody.'" Wiswall
soon promoted him to the jobbing department, a place
that took him all over young Chicago. What an eye for
business he had! Wiswall said, years later, "How well I
remember the boy! *Anxious to lay up money!* Exact and
economical! Just as zealous as a salesman, as he was later
a religious worker."

At first he found a boarding-place to his liking
with a Mrs. Phelps on North Michigan Avenue. Then
he moved into the shoe-store where several other
young fellows slept. (Chicago's primitive night-watchman
system.) Those Shoe Store Nights became the original
Chicago Forum where the youngsters had fiery debates
on nearly everything in politics and religion. Most of
them became lifelong friends, and some of them
would have made *Who's Who* had that Crimson
Egotism been published earlier: Ed Isham, Norman

Williams, Levi Leiter, (Gen.) G. W. Smith, (Gen.) J. L. Thompson, Benj. B. Page and William H. Seward!

In the spring of 1858, the twenty-one-year-old boy–"now fattened to one hundred and sixty"–got a real job, *Commercial Traveler* for C. N. Henderson. His travels took him at once, by all manner of transportation– steamboat, rig, horseback and train–all over the Middle West–Missouri, Iowa, Wisconsin, Nebraska, Indiana, Illinois. Letters in this period bear interesting references to the wild country, on which he saw "prairie fires, wolves, deers and prairie chickens thick as grasshoppers in August." On January 6, 1859, after less than a year in his new position, Henderson died; and a singular tribute was paid to the stripling just come of age, in that the estate of several hundred thousand dollars was turned over to him as administrator. Immediately, he entered the employment of Buell, Hill and Granger, but in a year he left them, as we shall see, for the greater firm of Christ and Church.

*   *   *

It is very interesting to observe how his commercial labors were supplemented by the service implied by his new life in Christ Jesus. He carried his church letter with him from Boston, in the striped carpet-bag. During October, 1856, he joined Plymouth Congregational Church, Rev. J. E. Roy, pastor. In November, his go-getter spirit led him to rent four pews, and to fill them with men and boys. Then he began to testify and lead in prayer. This didn't go so well. His Puritan habit of "shooting adjacent evil-doers while praying," was very disconcerting.

The temperature was a little low in Plymouth, therefore he sought new outlets. He found one in a group of young fellows in the First Methodist Episcopal Church. These boys had a "Mission Band" which made the rounds of saloons, hotels, and cheap lodging-houses, distributing tracts. In this capacity, March, 1857, he met J. B. Stillson, of Rochester, a witnessing layman, building the custom-house week-days, and on Sundays distributing tracts and holding meetings along the river.

One day in his shoe-jobbing tours, he saw a little Sunday school room on Chicago Avenue and Wells Street (just one block from the spot now occupied by the great herd of buildings called the Moody Bible Institute). The next Sunday he visited the school. I forgot the heat of a blistering July day in 1935, dreaming of the sheer romance of this boy asking for a class, and getting the reply that there were "twelve teachers and sixteen pupils, but, he could have any new scholars he brought in!" Then to see him the following Sunday report with eighteen bareheaded, barefooted, ragged, and dirty urchins, every one of them, as he explained, "with a soul to save." "He turned this class over to another to teach, and continued drumming up attendance until the school filled to overflowing." (Letter of Mrs. Moody, Washburne Collection).

While he himself never spoke to these boys about their souls—"that was the work of the elders, I thought"-it did determine his life. He wanted to get nearer where that sort lived. Well, there were plenty in Chicago's early Cicero-the rookeries in a shore section called "The Sands." In the blistering summer of 1858, he got together a class that he himself decided to teach; and met them for their first sessions on a drift-log beside Lake Michigan. And here we have the beginnings of the Moody Memorial Church![1]

By September, the class was too big for a log, so he rented an empty building, Corner of Illinois and Dearborn, once a saloon, but then too tumble-down even for that. It was fairly scandalous the way the thing grew. D. L. purchased a pinto pony, from a stranded cow person, and used it to promote attendance. It was a sight in those days to see him astride the pony while its back was filled, fore and aft, with ragamuffins-like an Austin crowded with sophomores. J. B. Stillson liked the school so well that he centered his work there.

And it kept growing. Mayor Haines gave him permission in November to take over, on Sundays, the North Market Hall, whose lower floor was a sort of free market, and whose upper floor was used week-nights for "the Devil's Revival" (a dance). He kept the saloon for prayer-meetings, and transferred his howling mob to the upper-floor dance-hall. There being no seats, they went Oriental, and

[1]There has been controversy as to whether the Beach Log Class was preliminary to the class in the Wells Street Mission which he turned over to another; or, to the saloon building mission. G. T. B. Davis' evidence decides it for me: "Behind the great building on North Avenue and Clarke Street was the group of boys on a log, with their spiritual Mark Hopkins."

sat on the floor. That's how the merchant prince, John Farwell, first saw them, and then bought the seats. When he went back the following Sunday to see how it looked, the noisy mob "whooped it up, and elected him superintendent by acclamation!"

"Crazy Moody"-that was his new name-flamed with growing enthusiasm. He and Stillson scoured "The Sands" for recruits. Within a year (1859) the attendance averaged six hundred, divided into eighty classes, one of which was taught by Emma. Then it jumped to a thousand, and sometimes fifteen hundred. Trudeau was the sweet singer. Somebody said of this roaring outfit: "Moody is the constitution, Stillson and Trudeau the by-laws." Its fame spread all over the Middle West; a curiosity, rivaling the stock-yards. And great business men like Col. C. G. Hammond attended "just to keep their hearts warm."

And it's hard to think that this mission work was merely a side-line, while Moody was still "working for a living over at Henderson's"; and good enough to draw several thousand a year for it. Moody's Mission went like a mill-race for six years in its two buildings, and then-well, that's another story.

*　　*　　*

On a hot July day in 1935, Deborah and I stood looking at the depressing, dilapidated prison on the corner of Dearborn and Illinois, standing where the North Market Hall once stood. Suddenly the roar of modern Chicago seemed to die away, and we were back in the days agone.

It was Thanksgiving night in the old saloon building. There were no gas-fixtures; just half a dozen candles "and the darkness had the best of it." We envisioned a group of shabby children gathered about him, while Moody sat with a candle in one hand, a Bible in the other and a child on his knee. Then he asked each one, "What are you thankful for?" It brings tears to one's eyes, and we're sure the angels rejoiced, as we seemed to hear over the years the shout of those "little ones of Christ,"

"There's nothin' we're so thankful for as *you*, Mr. Moody!"

MR. SHOE SALESMAN
(Washburne Collection)

Age twenty-five, when he removed his Bible school to
North Market Mission, 1857

VII
MR. SHOE SALESMAN BUCKLES ON THE SWORD OF EVANGEL
(March, 1860)

"I didn't know what this (personal work with members of a girls' class) was going to cost me. I was disqualified for business; it had become distasteful to me. I had got a taste of another world, and cared no more for making money. For some days after, the greatest struggle of my life took place. Should I give up business and give myself wholly to Christian work, or should I not? God helped me to decide aright, and I have never regretted my choice. O, the luxury of leading some one out of the darkness of this world into the glorious light and liberty of the gospel!"–*D. L. M. as quoted by the "Chicago Times Herald."*

Mr. Shoe Salesman Buckles on the Sword of Evangel
(March, 1860)

The blurred image which readers carry away from most of Moody's Lives is due to the fact that the writers considered his years to have had a uniform texture and quality. These biographers evidently imagined Moody's story could be filled in like a Mahomet's Bone Chest: something done now, lying next to something done twenty years later, which technique, to quote the careful imagery of Victor Hugo, resulted in structures exceedingly like "a feather on a pig's tail." A unique fact which grows upon critical analysis, is that Moody's life is a set of sharply defined endyses, each zone being of widely different quality, with a Dives gulf between. Slighting these phases has resulted, for instance, in making physical violence a part of Moody's *permanent* disposition, by citing the story of his manhandling roughneck hecklers in 1865. Such a thing could not happen after *The* Fire of 1871. Moody's life is like a series of Guided stones, built atop each other, and significant only when one refrains from getting the coarse concrete at the base mingled with the better granites just above. Naturally we would be surprised if the bush of the desert did not constantly change its very texture, a bit at a time, in response to the Abiding Fire.

The period of 1856 to 1859 is marked by two great passions which warred within him—the merchant and the missionary. It is fascinating to watch how the Salesman got covered up and finally lost forever in the rising tide of his evangelical fervor. He wanted to be rich; make lots of money. Of course! All his energies must be flanked in that direction. But his new heart in Christ Jesus had *something* to say about that. Surely, it was as honey in the comb to work in his mission to bring others to Christ. And it was the highest romance to be a business man part of the time, then to borrow Evangel's sword for a weekly flourishing. So he became a divided man, living a double life. And it should be said that he lived dangerously in both areas.

During the week, the boy covered, with seven-league boots, the raw territory of the ten Mid-Western States. Sales resistance was to him a lovely big hurdle to overleap. But on Saturdays, he put away his sample cases, and buckled on Evangel's sword. He just had to get back to Chicago! There was his beloved Mission; and there was Emma! . . To analyze how much was mission and how much was Emma, requires more wisdom than any of us, who have walked along the Same Dear Road, have ever received. One week in each month, his company allowed return fare on traveling expenses; the other Sundays were arranged on passes secured by Charles G. Hammond, Superintendent of the Chicago, Burlington and Quincy. But on Mondays D. L. changed his guise and "rattled back" (remember some of those old railroads, like the T. H. and P.?) to sell a

Hoosier frontiersman a bill of goods. This double life was great business!

But one day, as the old C. B. and Q. lurched south out of Galesburg, he found his heart was dying toward business. The missionary had overtopped the merchant. The Jekyll-Hyde shift had come to dreadful gear-clashing. Now that was serious. He was making *money*. The last eight months he set himself ahead $5000. He now had a total of $8000.[1]

The little English girl, Emma Charlotte Revell, in whom his interest was growing, had a curious attitude when he mentioned the problem to her: "*Money* isn't everything. What does *He* want you to do?" For nearly half a year his heart became a battle-ground; especially in the bumpy hours when he rode the pioneer trains out of Chicago Mondays; back Saturdays. For a man in that frame only a crisis could bring a conclusion. And the King Himself sent the crisis!

Moody's own account of it is the best narrative at this point.[2]

> "I had never lost sight of Jesus Christ since the first day I met Him in the store at Boston, but for years I really believed that I could not work for God. No one had ever asked me to do anything. When I went to Chicago, I hired four pews in a church, and used to go out on the street

[1]Statements here in hopeless variance, all the way from five to fifteen thousand dollars. Farwell says twelve thousand. Washburne fragments make me conclude eight.

[2]From a treasured, yellowed copy of the *Chicago Times-Herald*, Washburne Collection.

and pick up young men and fill these pews. I never spoke to those young men about their souls; that was the work of the elders, I thought. After working for some time like that, I started a mission Sabbath-school. I thought numbers were everything, so I worked for numbers. When the attendance ran below one thousand, it troubled me; and when it ran to twelve or fifteen hundred, I was elated. Still none were converted; there was no harvest.

"Then God opened my eyes. There was a class of young ladies in the school who were without exception the most frivolous set of girls I ever met. One Sunday the teacher was ill, and I took that class. They laughed in my face, and I felt like opening the door and telling them all to get out and never come back.

"That week the teacher of the class came into the store where I worked. He was pale, and looked very ill. 'What is the trouble?' I asked. 'I have had another hemorrhage of my lungs. The doctor says I cannot live on Lake Michigan, so I am going to New York State. I suppose I am going home to die.' He seemed greatly troubled, and when I asked the reason, he replied, 'Well, I have never led any of my class to Christ. I really believe I have done the girls more harm than good.' I had never heard anyone talk like that before, and it set me thinking. After awhile I said: 'Suppose you go and tell them how you feel. I will go with you in a carriage, if you want to go.'

"He consented, and we started out together. It was one of the best journeys I ever had on earth. We went to the house of one of the girls, called for her, and the teacher talked to her about her soul. There was no laughing then! Tears stood in her eyes before long. After he had explained the way of life, he suggested that we have prayer. He asked me to pray. True, I had never done such a thing in my life as to pray God to convert a young lady there and then. But we prayed, and God answered our prayer.

"We went to other houses. He would go up stairs, and be all out of breath, and he would tell the girls what he had come for. It wasn't long before they broke down and sought salvation. When his strength gave out, I took him back to his lodgings. The next day we went out again. At the end of ten days he came to the store with his face literally shining. 'Mr. Moody,' he said, 'the last one of my class has yielded herself to Christ.' I tell you we had a time of rejoicing.

"He had to leave the next night, so I called the class together that night for a prayer-meeting, and there God kindled a fire in my soul that has never gone out. The height of my ambition had been to be a successful merchant, *and if I had known that meeting was going to take that ambition out of me, I might not have gone.*

"But how many times I have thanked God since for that meeting! The dying teacher sat in the midst of his class and talked with them, and read the fourteenth chapter of John. We tried to sing 'Blest Be the Tie that Binds,' after which we knelt down to pray. I was just rising from my knees when one of the class began to pray for her dying teacher. Another prayed, and another, and before we rose *the whole class had prayed!* As I went out I said to myself, 'O God, let me die rather than lose the blessing I have received tonight!'

"The next evening I went to the depot to say good-bye to that teacher. Just before the train started, one of the class came, and before long, without any prearrangement, they were all there. What a meeting that was! We tried to sing, but we broke down. The last we saw of that dying teacher, he was standing on the rear car, his finger pointing upward, telling us to meet him in heaven."

Right here, behold a repetition of the Fascinated Young Man running to the Master, kneeling and sobbing "What must I do?" But in this case, when the Master said, "Leave all!" we are not called upon to view a sorrowful figure declining on account of possessions!

By this time (1860), Emma Revell had graduated from high school and was, at barely seventeen, a grammar school teacher. D. L.'s many Saturday returns to Chicago had made some very important changes. For one thing, *they were engaged!* To use the words of Emma's friend, Susannah Spurgeon, "loving looks, and tender tones and clasping hands gave way to verbal expression." But what a strange fiancée she was! She seemed to be tactfully pulling him to decide *against* business. Didn't she understand? Didn't she know it would mean poverty? What strange creatures these daughters of Eve are, anyway!

And on an early spring Saturday in 1860, as the old C. B. & Q. clicked back toward Chicago, "God helped me to decide aright!" After he had told *her,* he waited with anxiety for the quiet smile that came to her young face, a sign upon which he hung like a child for the next thirty-nine years. It was enough. Emma approved. What else mattered. He rushed over to B. F. Jacobs' establishment fairly shouting:

> "I have decided to give God all my time!"
> "How are you going to live?"
> "Well, God will provide for me if He wishes me to keep on; and I shall keep on until I am obliged to stop!"

His hire in the first year he committed himself to Evangel's sword was less than $300. But, the only *stop* his Lord ever commanded him to make was thirty-nine years later, when encircling angels came to bring him to the Gates of Glory.

CHRISTIANA
(Washburne Collection)

BRIDE AND GROOM
Emma (nineteen)　　　　　D. L. (twenty-five)
Married August 28, 1862

Emma Charlotte Revell
Born July 5, 1843; Died October 10, 1903

At twenty-five with her
daughter

At thirty-six when she became
a resident of Northfield

VIII
CHRISTIANA DELAYS NOT TO JOIN THE PROGRESS
(July 5, 1843–October 10, 1903)

If one's heart is tender, he cannot help being deeply moved at the sorrow of Bunyan's Pilgrim. When Charity asked him, "Why did you not bring your wife along with you?" he broke down and sobbed, "Oh, how willingly would I have done it, but she was averse to my going on pilgrimage!"

Moody never knew that heartbreak! For God gave him Emma Charlotte Revell! The little village paper of Northfield, dated October 17, 1903, carried a short obituary which puts the case in powerful simplicity:

"She found the greatest joy in the circle of her home and family, yet when duty called her to the responsibilities of social life, her natural grace and culture were admired by everybody. . . She made her home the best place on earth for her family. . . Everyone understood her wise counsel and support was one of the secrets of D. L. Moody's success."

And the closing sentence of that little article has an interpretative value, Dantesque in power–"Her flower-covered bier was borne to Round Top and her body placed beside that of her husband."

Why not? That's exactly where she was from first to last,–*beside her husband!–Sketch Book.*

CHRISTIANA DELAYS NOT TO JOIN
THE PROGRESS
(July 5, 1843-October 10, 1903)

The staff of the Chicago Historical Society furnished along with other valued data for this book, the picture facing page 66, which helps imagination restore the downtown Chicago of Moody's arrival. Note the water-carts, "hoss-cars," gigs, rigs, hoop-skirts and "tails." Here we are, right on Washington and La Salle Streets. The large building on the left, Ladies and Gentlemen, is the City Hall, famous throughout the new West. Today, the bastile granite of the new City Hall stands on the same lot. Now, attention please! The building in picture center *is* the Chamber of Commerce; but *it was the edifice of the First Baptist Church.*

After purchasing it for sixty thousand dollars in 1862, the Chamber of Commerce razed the twin corner towers, and changed the Baptist Meeting-house into a "Temple of Talk," where early boosters waxed eloquent over "Half a Century of Progress." The same site is today occupied by the Babel-high structure of the Foreman State National Bank Building.

It helps a bit, to get such a flash back on the March of Time, for it was in front of that middle center building, on Sunday, September 16, 1856, while it was still the First Baptist Church, that young Moody

89

stopped, went in-and was conquered. An early morning rain had deluged the streets, followed by autumn sunshine. After the boy sat down, and during the opening exercises of the Sunday school, it wasn't long before he saw-a girl. She had all that unspoiled sweetness of thirteen, which made the poet pray, "God keep her so young, so lovely, so fine!" It must be confessed that several times before service-end there was that "embarrassing, yet delightful collision of eyes." And the girl, of course, was-Emma Charlotte Revell.

*   *   *

Reverently, this chapter aims to enter the shadows which a century has dropped about this woman, knowing that human appraisals have never done her justice, hoping that Centennial year will put her where she belongs-among the Historic Wives of the Faith. Only the Recording Angel knows how completely the regimentation of that raw explosive called D. L. M. was due to the quiet spirituality, calm common sense, and fine British restraint of Emma Charlotte Revell. But even as it was with her friend Susannah Spurgeon, her age dismissed her with a paragraph.

John Foster's impatience with historians, all of whom gave only cheese-paring and candle-end data upon King Alfred's Life, is matched by my own pucker against *every one* of Moody's biographers. Foster's indictment nicely sums up the case of Mrs. Dwight L. Moody versus the Guild of Cacoëthes Scribendi: "One is indignant at them for having given so meager an outline. Their short imperfect relations and descriptions are like ruins of a once majestic temple, where are seen only such vestiges of the foundations as to show the magnitude of the plan."

Amazed at this literary silence, Deborah and I counted upon finding adequate details in the public records of Northfield. Alas! Only a little column in the Press of October 17, 1903! Then said Deborah, "Just wait till we get to Chicago." But the yellowed files of the Lake City groaned, and brought forth only a mouse-article twenty-seven lines long, including the heads.

However, Mrs. D. L. Moody's letters and comments in the Washburne Collection, like a few broken columns, intimate to the imagination the beauty and richness of her life and labors. Her father, Fleming H. Revell, left England and emigrated to Chicago in 1849, because, to be frank about it, he heard there was good going on Lake Michigan in the building of side-wheelers and wind-jammers. And he was somewhat in the way of being a ship-builder himself. (You know the deprecatory, shyly coughing manner in which Britons speak of themselves.) Mr. Charles Revell Holden, Chicago, writes me September, 1935:

> "My grandfather (Fleming Revell) died ten years before I was born. I recall a typical portrait of a typical English gentleman. My grandmother (Emma's mother) lived to be over eighty years of age, and was a fine lovable character."

This vignette outline enables us to see these Spurgeon-Baptist Revells, as they arrived in Pinafore Chicago, with their three young daughters. Anna and Sara were eight and four respectively; Emma, six, was born July 5, 1843. Winsome little misses every one of them, as anybody with half an eye can see from their pictures.

Follow on a line or so. On December 11, 1849, a son was born in Chicago, Fleming H. (II). At twenty this son launched *his* ship on a sea of printer's ink, publishing first an "itsy bitsy" religious pulp, *Everybody's Paper,* adding after the Big Fire *Words of Life, Sunday School Illustrator,* etc. The first book he printed was Mackey's *Grace and Truth.* Just as Passmore and Alabaster were "made" by Spurgeon, Revell saw his airy little business jump to gianthood when his famous brother-in-law, D. L. Moody, rubbed the lamp with the Colportage Library. Today, the grandson, Fleming H. Revell (III) has a nice little office on a nice little street called Fifth Avenue, New York City.

All of which may help explain the patrician fineness of the thirteen-year-old Emma Charlotte, in whom the nineteen-year-old Moody found himself "spürlos versenkt"! What an adorable little lady she was, with her dark eyes, clean-cut features, British refinement, and best of all, ardent passion to lead others to her young King! They *saw* each other that day but they were not formally *introduced* until the following May. (Can you recall the lovely suspense of those delicate formalities which this sad age has lost?)

By the time she was fifteen, D. L.'s mission was a lusty creature packed full of embryonic gangsters. Is it hard to understand why she "went over and took a class"? Not very. At no other point is the Unreasonable Grace of God more to be observed than when He brought this adorable young lady into Moody's life. More and more the boy and the girl found love's sweet reasons for being together, until one day the twenty-three-year-old shoe salesman said a certain something to the seventeen-year-old girl, which every man who finds his woman knows perfectly well. And she, slipping her slender hand into his, whispered Ruth's avowal:

> "Where thou goest I will go,
> Where thou lodgest, I will lodge!"

The following Sunday she blushed when her rough-cut lad announced in the mission,

"I've just become engaged to Miss Emma Revell, and please don't count on me to see the girls home from meeting any more!"

There's a letter in the Washburne Collection under date of August 23, 1862, that sounds like a lover's hallelujah. It is headed, "Him that trusteth in me shall not be confounded" (!) and it runs:

> "DEAR SAMUEL: By the time you get this, I shall be married and away on my wedding *tower*!" (Italics mine.)

They were married in the First Baptist Church, August 28, 1862, by Dr. W. W. Everts, pastor. The bride's dark hair was partly caught up in a coil at the back of her head, the remainder falling over her shoulders right and left in clusters of curls. A perforated pearl clasp joined her white lace collar ends, matching white lace epaulettes over a snug, black velveteen bodice, completed by an ankle-length skirt of the same material—"a little lady whose slenderness made her seem quite tall." And the groom! Ah my friends, remember, he was a sort of a preacher, now. So, who can have the heart to speak unkindly of the solid-black Prince Albert, matching the black, string tie, black side-burns and hair? And why can't Love's Young Dream permit a man at least *once* in his life to pose with a hand on his hip, and the other on a table-borne Bible? Dear me, if we're normal people, our laughter cannot help being sweetened with tears!

Thus began another of those transforming homes, wherein the wife was well-content to mother her largest boy, *her husband,* and to abide, unobserved, in the shadow of his labors. A hundred times I've said to people who ought to have known, "Tell me about Mrs. Moody." And just as often, like sainted Doctor Gray, they've acted confused and finally said, *"Well-she was very quiet!"* She deliberately hid herself. But I've run so many transit-lines across her character that she has become as real to me as her husband. Her modesty was copied from Another, but as for her real self this age must know that here was "One of the notable women to whom the nations come!" As I have grieved over not finding Spurgeon's "Little Black Book," so do I regret that Emma Charlotte Revell's diary is locked away. . .

Happily, though, there are enough dots on the page to connect by a proper line and thus draw out a vital picture. The sum total of her influence over the Commoner of Northfield was exceeded by that of but One Other. John Bunyan described his heroine as delaying to join the Progress; but here was a Christiana who *thrust* her Pilgrim forth, and then, walked *by his side* clear to the gates of glory!

After the wedding, they moved into their first house, "Poverty Cottage," at Dearborn and Indiana. (What honest man's eyes can be dry at the memory of this sweet discipline?) Just to see her, uncomplainingly walking through the first desert years of young married life is to think of Jeremiah 2:2:

> "I remember thee, . . the love of thine espousals, when thou wentest after me . . . in a land that was not sown."

At first she was proud but alarmed by her husband's intense activities. Then she mastered the dextrous art which she applied the rest of her life. "She has been at his side as it were a brake upon this impetuous man, and held him back and guarded him all through these years" (Ira D. Sankey).

Three times she made the Woman's Pilgrimage of Pain, and came back holding tiny little hands-Emma (Mrs. A. P. Fitt), 1864; William Revell, 1869; and Paul, 1879. Her mother-love captivated Jessie McKinnon: "Often during meetings (in

England) she remained at home with her children (Emma and Will) and it was beautiful to see her devotion." Yes, and it was beautiful when she, teaching them daily to pray, would say, "O my little dears, you belong body and soul to Christ!"

In those early days she continued to work in her husband's mission. There is that engaging story of a distressed visitor who saw "an altogether-too-young girl" teaching a class of men in the gallery; and whose complaints were finally quieted by D. L.'s telling him, "Well, she's my *wife!*" In the quietness of her home she often talked to D. L. about England, its beauty, but chiefly of the mighty men of the Book who lived there. Finally, in 1867, five years after they were married, D. L. made an abrupt announcement to his Sunday school, an announcement combining business and pleasure: His wife had asthma; a doctor said an ocean trip might cure her; and therefore they were going to England that week. (And-page Ripley-it *did* cure her.)

The Washburne Collection shows by little fragments that she was throughout life his constant companion almost everywhere he went, even to the front in the Civil War:

FORTRESS MONROE
MAR. 10, 1864

MY DEAR BRO. SAMUEL

You will see by this date that I am on my way agane to Gen Grants army. *My wife is with me* (Italics mine) she will have to hurry back home for the child (Emma) is not with us.

Together they visited the shrines of faith in Europe. There is a letter in her own dainty hand which says they went to the quaint old home of John Knox where she and "D. L. *both* rested in an old chair belonging to him." Other letters give charming little cameos of herself and D. L. at teas, religious gatherings, pleasure drives, tête-à-têtes with Europe's great men, ten days at the Paris Exposition. . .

In the later sixties, the young couple got along a little better financially. Their joy was full on New Year's Day, 1871. A friend of D. L. had just built a row of new Chicago houses, fire-fodder of sardine uniformity. One was set aside, rent-free, for the Moodys. Other friends of the mission had furnished it—Brussels carpets, great bookcase with glass doors, circular-burner kerosene-lamp with a Mandarin-white glass shade, and on one wall a heroic-sized oil-painting of D. L. On that New Year's Day, the three Moodys (little Emma just seven) were picked up by a carriage. They found the new house full of friends *laughing* over something or other. Then Doctor Patterson pompously presented the young couple with a key, a lease to the house, and all it contained, as a gift. D. L., confused, gave the key to Emma. Hand-in-hand they went through the rooms. D. L. tried to make a speech, broke down, and Emma had to finish it for him. Within a few months, October 8, 1871, the line of fire-fodder houses went up like tinder in the Great Holocaust. About the only thing Emma showed any anxiety about saving was the oil-painting of D. L.

"D. L." as the focal center of her life, crops out continually in her letters–"D. L.–D. L.–D. L.!"

174 GT. WESTERN ROAD
GLASGOW, APRIL 19, 1882

DEAR BROTHER ED:

> . . . You will be glad to know that D. L. though working hard is *very well*. . . He has been very much blessed in Glascow. . . He is now preaching in a very poor district in Glascow. . . It makes my heart ache to see the wretchedness there, and it is most of it caused by drink. . . People in Northfield hardly imagine such wretchedness. . . Fannie and Emma have gone to the seacoast to get a breath of fresh air; and they will get it,–pretty direct from the north pole! Dr. Blaikie has a *summer* residence right on the shore! . . Last Saturday, D. L. and I went with a gentleman to . . . an immense castle on the Clyde, with most beautiful grounds . . . furnished beautifully . . . marble statues and paintings . . . we are driving to some lovely Scotch lakes. . .

The affection between her husband and Spurgeon was reflected in the love between herself and Susannah Spurgeon. When the Heir of the Puritans died, Mrs. Spurgeon sent to the Moodys in Northfield, a priceless book (I'd give every volume in my library to own it), the Bible in which Spurgeon had noted down, as he preached them, each theme properly enmargined and dated, his 3,517 sermons. In

1884, Mrs. Moody and her daughter, then a young lady of twenty, spent the winter in Mentone. Spurgeon was there; Susannah had become the helpless invalid in Westwood. Emma's heart went out toward the sorrowing Puritan; was not D. L. his Jonathan? And one day when Spurgeon wept over his stricken loved one, Emma turned her lovely eyes toward the great preacher and whispered, "Through fire and water I have brought thee into a large place."

*   *   *

The flying years became laden with rich argosies of memory for the Moodys. The current of his love toward her deepened, becoming as he drew near sixty, a more exalted thing than even the adoration his heart accorded the little lady of Chicago so many years agone. And why not? Her love for him never made her a mere unthinking echo of a great man, but always spoke out in British independence, shearing away many rough spots, and heaven knows he had plenty. There was, for instance, the time when Moody was still "a hook-up preacher" (one who hooks together a quantity of material he likes, and then to give it a religious semblance, tacks a text to it). When D. L. asked her how she liked the preaching of Henry Moorhouse, she replied, "Very, very much. He's so *different* from you. *He* backs up everything he *says* with the Bible!"

In the Inquiry Room, she was superb. Moody often said, "She can bring a man to Christ when I cannot touch him"; and he handed the hard cases over to her. Ramshorn (E. P.) Brown was one of her many trophies. The fact that Moody Church has always had a baptistry in it was due, not to A. C. Dixon, as the good dominie imagined, but to Moody's wife who never gave over her Baptist convictions.

She handled the larger part of D. L.'s correspondence; was his constant adviser. But she knew just where to stop, never crossing that mystic boundary where Mrs. True Helpmeet becomes Madame Married Interference. When questions came which Moody should settle on his own Guidance, she replied to his excited "What shall I do?" with, "You decide, and tell *me* and I'll *write*." Jessie McKinnon, brilliant young wife of a British steamship magnate, was awed by Emma's "humility, her great nobility of character, her sincerity and transparency. I am convinced that a great deal of Mr. Moody's usefulness is owing to her."

When the Moodys became permanent residents of Northfield, in 1876, D. L.'s cup of joy ran over, and the children shared his enthusiasm. But as for Emma, well, the night silence of a country village made even the crickets sound like Squakeags come back for a war-dance; and that distressing smalltown talk—you know, "Alexander's cat has kittens" or "Mercy Mudge trimmed over that old black leghorn"—it just didn't appeal to a woman with a city background. There were many lonesome hours for her in this New England Nazareth when she longed for the uproar of young Chicago's giant forces.

But her affections slowly rooted more deeply into New England than in the soil of Cook County. The sweet harmony of Northfield years flowed like a glorious river until that dark day in December, 1899. Life then suddenly lost its savor. Little did friends know that when they put him on Round Top they buried her heart, too.

One day, a few months after D. L.'s home-going, conscious that the shadows of her own final sickness were falling, she stood, ending a visit with the beloved physician and his wife, those last lonely moments of tarrying at their veranda door. To look upon her one would say, "She's the same royal person save that the dreams in her eyes have turned to memories." Tears just would come as she gazed westward over the Great Meadow beside the river. How precious D. L. had been to her! No wonder sister Sara said to the reporters, "They were so poor when they were married! But they were so happy! And that happiness continued throughout their lives."

Yes, she loved England with its December roses, and Chicago of radiant morning memories; but, after all, this quiet paradise on the Connecticut was the best. Maybe, because *he* loved it; and her heart always played such queer tricks of loving what he loved. She became strangely silent. Doctor Wood and his wife understood, and were silent with her.

Her lonely heart was listening to a dying man calling his departed grandchildren, "Dwight! Irene! I see the children's faces!" She listened more closely for memory to repeat certain sweet words that she had lingered over every day during those lonely two years, the last words he ever said before he shouted his praise in the presence of the King:

"Emma, you've been a *good* wife to me!" He had said just that. Dear God, what lovelier thing did a man ever say to a woman!

It was to her a welcome moment on October 10, 1903, when she closed her eyes to the autumn gold of New England, and opened them to the gold of the City Four-Square. Doctor Wood and his five helpers, H. M. Moore, H. W. Pope, S. E. Bridgeman, Deacon Barker, and H. H. Proctor, placed her body beside her husband's on Round Top. Yea, verily, and that's where she belongs, now, and on Resurrection morn.

*   *   *

I have desired to carve yet another text upon her stone, the poignantly sweet words of the Shunammite,

"I dwell among my people!"

IX
PILGRIM WALKS IN THE FLESH
(March, 1860–October, 1871)

We now regard the bewildering interval in Pilgrim's life when his labors savor of animal heat. Apollos is eloquent, mighty and diligent; but he knows only the baptism of John. His bold speaking has a Delphic sound to everybody—save Aquila and Priscilla. This is the same amazing interlude when the contemporary prophet cherishes his Circular Club, is a Bright Eyed Boy for the Chamber of Commerce, liberally quotes the poetry of Ætna St. Hoi Polloi, and pants over wide orbits to declare his soul on a warless world. If this fitful fever is cured by Divine Prescription, he repents of it all just as he repented of his sins. If the violence of fire (Hebrews 11:34) is quenched by natural decline, our Peppy Prodigy cools down to a Gray Gibeonite, hewing wood and drawing water.

Such, by the large, was Moody in the decade 1860-1870. What Marathon exhibitions! What breath-taking activities! Of course there was much to admire, and much good came of it. But, he was not yet *The Burning Bush* whom the world turned aside to see.—*Sketch Book.*

PILGRIM WALKS IN THE FLESH
(March, 1860–October, 1871)

The labors of Moody in his twenties have a Paul Bunyan flavor. After days of research one watches the record of this Hercules become oppressively bulky, and then wonders: How can it all be packed into a Life? These remarkable conversions, wholesale philanthropies, battle-front dramas and seven-league-convention travels? Well, that's just what should *not* be done. Spiritual Horatio Algers have in the past led us astray by attempting it. To such writers the Moody of the sixties was a faultless Galahad whose every move is to be studied, moralized upon, and imitated. Just to read their books is to feel beaten with rods into admitting that faith is after all merely another word for furious pottering.

This is precisely where Gamaliel Bradford got all at sea in his Irritated Biography. Offended by the wild, driving haste of Moody, he concluded "The hurried man" of this period to be Moody, clear to the end of the picture; this man who had no time to read or even to think; this man who rushed through life making felonious assaults upon total strangers with his rude challenge "Are you a Christian?"[1] The author of "Damaged Souls" was overwhelmed because he seems never so much as to have heard

[1] The annals of the sixties offer copious proof that this "rudeness" was honored, however. Many men, writhing as they at first thought, in indignation, found later the arrows of God, not young Moody, had wounded them.

105

of the fathomless difference between a Christian "born again" only, and the same Christian after Jehovah has made him a Polished Shaft. The difference one may see between Impulsive Simon, who cut off policemen's ears, and Dynamic Peter, whose, reins were in the hands of God. If one does not sense the question, "On which side of Whitsunday was Moody then living?" he of course must write as a man with a measuring-line.

This period is filled with stories of life-changing that belong to the literature of power; the records of men, enchained of soul by all forms of sin, from gutter bestiality to sleek, moral rebellion, suddenly moved upon by the Spirit and made new creatures in Christ Jesus. But the motif of this Life forces us to shelve these stirring anecdotes with sincere regret. The highest blessing for any young heart, anxious for His dear sake to receive power in this age, will be to watch attentively how the Long-Suffering Potter took the violent clay called D. L. and disciplined it into a humble vessel fit to receive "This Treasure."

*　　*　　*

About 1860 Major D. W. Whittle had a distinct impression that Moody was a little off, "the newspapers were full of jokes about him, and folks called him Crazy Moody." The first time Whittle ever saw him, he was riding a small pony, trousers in his boot-legs, cap on his head, a short stocky figure. A little later he went ministerial, even returning to Northfield, in 1862, for a visit, dressed in a Prince

Albert, his bearing marked by lofty meekness of a very young clergyman. By 1870 he was no longer stocky, just (as prosaic tailors say) a short stout. And since Spurgeon, to whom he was a Jonathan, had a full beard, Moody had one also. A contemporary gives this little cameo: "I never saw such high pressure; he made me think of those breathing steamboats on the Mississippi that must go fast or burst: a keen, dark-eyed man with a shrill voice, and a thorough earnestness." Moody himself, while regarding these years as exhibiting "zeal without knowledge," often added, "But there is much more hope for a man in that condition than for that man who has knowledge without zeal."

*　　*　　*

The Civil War roared down on America in April, 1861. A mobilization center, Camp Douglas, was located in the quail-hunters' paradise south of Chicago (just about where the University of Chicago now stands). As the first regiment of soldiers was arriving, D. L. and the Y. M. C. A. Devotional Committee, of which he was chairman, were on the grounds pitching a big tent for an evening prayer-service. This was followed by a chapel financed and built by Moody. During the war over 1,500 gospel services were held in Camp Douglas. "Moody was ubiquitous; hastening from one barracks to another, day and night, week-days and Sundays; praying, exhorting, conversing with men about their souls, reveling in the abundant work and swift success the war brought within his reach."

The famous Christian Commission, a sort of combination Red Cross and Y. M. C. A., was set up with George H. Stuart, of Philadelphia, General Chairman. Many of Moody's letters in the Washburne Collection are written on this stationery, which prints his name on prominent committees. In this connection he went ten times to the war front; four years of back and forth; on battle-fields just after or during engagements–Pittsburg Landing, Shiloh, Fort Donelson, Murfreesboro–preaching to great crowds, visiting the wounded, working among the soldiers. When the Confederacy crashed, he was among the first to enter Richmond, "ministering to friend and foe alike." All of these experiences were later to have high value. He could always hear, "the dying groans of the men and their call for water; and it made him think of the sufferings of Another." And, as he told these stories to assembled thousands, their sobs bore proof that they, too, heard and thought.

*   *   *

We hasten to affirm that an adequate concept of Moody demands a steel-engraving page, picturing his Y. M. C. A. activities. Like a steel-engraving, this aspect must be concisely drawn, a true picture in quick, short lines. All burdensome minutiæ must be rigidly rubbed out to relieve the eye of confusing detail. There is no better place to discuss Moody and the Association than right here, and then have done with it. Therefore, this mosaic chip draws color from beyond the limits of the chapter.

On one hand, the Association did "more in developing him for service than any other."[2] On the other, Moody did more for the Association than it did for him. From the solid edifice in San Francisco to the buildings in Boston, from Cheviot Hills to John O'Groat's in Britain's Tight Little Islands, there are scores of units immeasurably indebted to Moody.

It is very hard to examine the Association of today, and find the reasons for Moody's enthusiasm. One could not do this unless he looked over the "Y" magazines of fifty years ago, such as *The Watchman*. At once he finds that in Moody's day, the Y. M. C. A. had "the ancient fire by which whole shoals of martyrs once did burn." *Then*, it was Bible study, personal evangelism, Bible conference, testimony meetings, Bible exposition, street-preaching. Today, the Association, with its Athenian buildings, is doing just what Moody feared, "carrying dead men" (unconverted workers). A guarded breadth has replaced Bible enthusiasm; its leaders seem content in rushing youth around and around, out of the gym and into the night-school, out of the pool and into the ridotto. If one seeks a real aid today in providing valuable spiritual training for youth-soul, he must look elsewhere.

The Association had its origin in a little London back room where some clerks, George Williams, leader, held prayer-meetings, and finally, June 6, 1844, took the name, "London Young Men's Chris-

[2]W. R. Moody quotes his father in the revised biography, Macmillan, 1931.

tian Association." Washburne Collection letters show Moody enjoying reading-hours in a Boston branch as early as 1854. The revival of 1857 washed the "Y" into Chicago. It ran well for a while, then languished, being captured by old men.

Then came Moody with a bang, bang! As Chairman of the Association Relief Committee, in 1858, "he rode his pinto in the visitation of 554 families during the year. He practically took over the noon prayer-meeting of the early sixties, and made it electric with bold attacks on "professors who tippled, used tobacco, went to the theatre, played billiards and other loaferish games. Should Christians be silent about such matters? No! a thousand times, No!" The prayer-meeting, overcrowded at once, had to be moved to a large, back room in the Methodist Church Block. By 1865 he was inescapable, so they made him president.

The Methodist Hall was now too small, so he organized a stock company "to build a large and handsome hall." John Farwell, at Moody's suggestion, gave the lot (in the Loop) on which his home stood, as a building site. The $100,000 edifice with its 3,000-seat auditorium was dedicated September 29, 1867. In his address, Moody said, "When I see young men by the thousands going in the way of death, I feel like falling at the feet of Jesus with prayer and tears to come and save them. This (building) is His answer. I have faith that a mighty influence will go out from us that shall help bring the whole world to God."

In January, 1868, "the glorious building burned"!

Before the ruins stopped smoking the Chicago Trio, Moody, Farwell, and B. T. Jacobs began a campaign to build another edifice. Farwell Hall number two became "a towering religious center, with a soul in sympathy with every Godly work, and a mother of revivals." The noon prayer-meetings, preceded by D. L.'s own hour in the closet under the stairs, became Pentecostal.

And Farwell the second burned in October, 1871.

We understand by this glance into yesterday why Moody constantly linked the momentum of his revivals here and in England to pull Associations out of debt and erect new buildings. There was open vision in *those* days.

*   *   *

Another "side line" of the decade was his activity in general Sunday school conventions. Prior to the war, he gained some degree of publicity through a program collapse in Princeton, Illinois, March, 1861. The "distinguished speakers" failed to arrive-too much blizzard. In despair the committee turned to Moody and E. W. Hawley (a young dry-goods merchant) to pinch-hit. The pair arrived in Princeton too late to go to bed and too early to sit up. Shivering with the combined cold of zero weather and program-fright, they spent the night in intercession. The next day they scrapped the brain-trust program, and "went in for meetings with an inquiry room." A lusty revival broke out all over Bureau County.

Right after the war, Moody said to Farwell and Jacobs, "The war's ended. Let's give our strength to Sunday school work." The second Illinois State Association was announced to begin the first Tuesday in March, 1864, in Springfield. Moody and Rev. J. F. Harwood, the "pastor of Moody Mission" (really associate to D. L.) went down to the Capital City the Friday night preceding "to see if a convention could be made something beside a parade. Was it wrong to have a pre-convention to this end? No! a thousand times, No!" By the time the delegates arrived Moody had again "stolen the picture," and the town was in a revival. The delegates returned home, not to report mildly on the scientific pedagogic, but to "Bring them in from the folds of sin!"

From this point on, Moody was not to be ignored; to be eyed at first suspiciously by his brethren, then received into power. The record of these activities in the next seven years sound like a full-time secretary's work. Repeated gatherings all the way from Du Quoin to Quincy: "the progress of these two brethren (Moody and William Reynolds of Peoria) was a sort of triumphal procession; large numbers of people accompanying them in wagon and on horseback; open-air meetings, tent meetings, field meetings, street meetings." Time fails to speak of Decatur, Danville, Cairo, *and Boston*–where he stopped the mouths of program lions, and obtained a good report through faith.

*   *   *

It is a relief to find we are about finished with these records of exalted monotony—"great meetings, great labors." One area more—the embryo church of which he was lay pastor, *the* work his soul really loved.

It was during his heavy side-lines incident to war activities that he set about the task of building an edifice better suited to the needs of his school than the North Market Hall and the old saloon. In 1863, a lot was secured on Illinois Street, between Wells and La Salle Streets, and a new building, the Illinois Street Church, was completed in November at a cost of $20,000. "A two-story gable-end edifice, main front door in the middle, spindling corner spires, tiny Colonial tower on the comb, with an American flag."

At first the converts were urged to unite with "regular orthodox churches." Then the growth was so rapid that organization became imperative. A denominational council was called: each representative wanted Moody to organize in the form of his own denomination. Moody ended by making it nominally Congregational, though totally independent of even that body. It adopted rigidly orthodox "Articles of Faith" upon such items as the Trinity, the Scripture, the Fall of Man, the Person, Work, Death and Resurrection of Christ. Also a conventional set-up of officers.[3] And in this building the vigorous four hundred kept open shop, night and day, until October, 1871. The portrayal of his divine fury, the purpose of this chapter, is best

[3]See Daniels' *D. L. Moody*, Chapter VIII.

accomplished by quoting, in his own words and spelling, certain of his letters from the Washburne Collection:

"Jany 13 1862 Dear Brother   The happiest howers I have ever spent on earth are in Sunday School Samuel get a class of wicked boys find some very bad boys & get them to Sunday School & then ask God to give you wisdom and Instruct them in the way of Eternal Life."   (He had been married only a few months when this letter was written. The "happiest hours" therefore, were largely the ones when, still single, he had no income, was obliged to give up his lodging house, sleep on association benches, and live on cheese and crackers.)

"Hudson R bet N Y & Albany, July 17, 1862 My Dear Bro Samuel   I have wondered if you have done as I am ancious to have you do in regard to connecting your self with Sunday School. . . O Samuel you don't know how much you mite be able to do if you will only trye."

"Chicago April 11, 1863 Dear Bro Samuel   The school is nearly 2 as large as it was when you was hear. . . What is to hender you from having a Sunday School in the school house. . . God will help you do it. . . Start one and love the children and they will gather round you. . . Enclosed you will find a card which every child in my Sunday School has one & when he comes I punch out a number & with that card I can tell how regular

he comes through the Qurter." (The tiny green card lies on my desk: a sacred bit of pasteboard.)

"*Chicago Oct 28, 1863* Dear Bro & Mother My new building (the Illinois Street Chapel) is doing first rate. I think they will have the roof on this week" (This building, the "Illinois Street Chapel," soon to become a full-fledged church, was erected at a cost of $20,000.00-collected by D. L. himself!)

"*Chicago Jany 22 1864* Dear Bro Samuel You and Lizzie ought to unite yourself with some church it belongs to the Lord "Jesus" Only think of the number fallen into the grave and nothing done to reach them go seek them and build up the Sunday School and get Eliza Lyman to take hold with you. My hart bleeds for my natave town."

"*Chicago June 9, 1865*   I hope I may be kept humble!" (And it was in this interval that Hercules made extra flourishes such as making two hundred calls in one day-one and a half minutes to each: a feat of flesh-work not to be admired or imitated.)

* * *

A general picture of his hurried life is drawn by himself in another priceless letter:

"*Chicago Jan 13 1862*

Dear Bro What am I doing this winter . . . I am agent for the City Relief Society that takes care of the poor. . . I have some 500 or 800 people dependent on me for their daily food. . . I keep a Sadall horse to ride around with & then I Keepe a nother horse & man to waite on the folks as they come to my office I make my head quarters in the roomes of the Y. M. C. A. I have just raised money enough to erect a chappell for the soldiers at the camp 3 miles from the city I hold a meeting down there every day & 2 in the city. So you see I have 3 meetings to attend to every day besides calling on the sick & that is not all I have to go into the country about every wek to buy wood & provisions . . . also coal wheat meal & corn then I have to go hold meetings like 36 miles just to one prayer meeting at Elgin I am also raising money to buy Him books for the Soldiers I am one of the Army Commity & we hold meetings once a week . . . and then distribute books to the diferunt Companys. . . I do not ansur 1 letter out of 10 that I get It is 11 to 12 every night when I retire and am up in the morning at light. Wish you would come in sometime about 1 to 3 o'clock my office hours & see the people waiting *I do not get 5 minutes a day to study so I have to talk just as it happens*" (Italics mine).

*   *   *

Ah, here is the small black spot that spread and got him in the end,—"not five minutes a day . . so I have to talk just as it happens"! It was inevitable that a man, though in the service of God, who let his life go to this point, should eventually sense futility. It began to darken his soul by 1866. Something *was* wrong! He now faced that spiritual crisis involving an entire revolution in character, which a writer sets forth in the phrase,

> "They made me keeper of the vineyards;
> But mine own vineyard have I not kept."

X
AND HIS WORKS BECOME BONDAGE
(March, 1860–October, 1871)

Now Pilgrim came to such a frame that he was always ill at ease. He looked into the gloom of his soul and was amazed to find that his unrest arose from the performance of the very work for which he so stoutly affirmed his love. Thus he came to a deep sense of shame. Then one day he found in the message sent out week by week, by the man who lived beneath The Shadow of the Broad Brim, a clear discernment of his whole trouble: "I am bound to say, if Christ's servant be not in the power of the Spirit, then His works become bondage, and he feels forced to do them."

Forthwith Pilgrim began to pray, "Oh God! give me the Holy Spirit!"–*Sketch Book.*

AND HIS WORKS BECOME BONDAGE
(March, 1860-October, 1871)

It is a dreadful experience to become an Ahimaaz, running without a commission; to have a well-meaning heart and an impoverished soul. To feel the hand of God lying heavily upon the spirit–that dreadful period in which Mr. Ordinary Christian must writhe in anguish until Christ be formed within. By the year 1867 the consciousness of something wrong blackened his whole outlook. To meet the unidentified malady he plunged into the chasm Santayana described, "Redoubling one's efforts when he's losing his vision." More furious he became, and more unhappy. Emma viewed his misery with unveiled eyes; she knew what the real trouble was. Therefore, she plied a woman's sweet ministry of talk: they might go to England for a visit; there were such giants of God's word there; it would be a great blessing to D. L.; the Plymouth Brethren in Chicago had gotten their priceless secrets from Spirit-filled English Christians. There were other men in England like C. H. McIntosh and J. N. Darby whose books had so blessed him. . .

Here we find the real reason for the first English visit, March to July, 1867. There seemed to have been no extensive planning, just that abrupt announcement that an ocean-trip might help his loved companion. But the deepest motivation was his anxiety to cure his own *spiritual* asthma (not Emma's), by contact with British men of the Book.

The sum total result of this trip was transforming, *but it was not transfiguring.*

For one thing, he was permitted to hear the young man preach who, next to Christ, had been his ideal for ten years—Charles Haddon Spurgeon. Spurgeon was then thirty-three, Moody thirty.

> "The very first place to which he went in London was Metropolitan Tabernacle. He was surprised one had to have a ticket to get in, but he got in just the same. He had read every thing Spurgeon ever wrote. He sat weeping during the service and his eyes just feasted on Spurgeon. While he (Moody) remained in England in 1867, he followed Spurgeon everywhere. When he got home, people asked him if he had been to see this or that Cathedral; he had to say, 'No,' but he could tell them all about *Mr. Spurgeon!* He just couldn't keep back the tears when he thought of it. He would like to buy the seat in the high gallery where he was first seated, and take it back to America with him. It was Bethel to him, and he went home a better man." [1]

But, *that wasn't enough!*

He also made a close study of that miracle of faith, George Müller, and from that time on Müller's *Autobiography* became Moody's *Pilgrim's Progress.*

[1] Moody's speech at Spurgeon's Jubilee, 1884. Quoted from *Spurgeon's Autobiography*, Judson Press.

But, *that wasn't enough!*

During this first visit also he met in Dublin the "puny, fragile, provincial and rude-speeched young Harry Moorhouse,"[2] who followed Moody back to Chicago and became God's instrument for changing Moody's whole concept of preaching. After Moorhouse's brief and spectacular ministry in Chicago in 1867, Moody had no need of further proof that a Christian must first know precisely what the Bible *says*, before he is at all competent to explain what it *teaches!* Of which, this book has more to say in Chapter XVI.

But, that wasn't enough!

Moody was only theoretically convinced. It's labor unto blood to do real scriptural preaching! Old Man Inertia got Moody after Moorhouse left, and he went on with his sawdust homiletics. It is true that when he returned to Chicago in 1867 everybody could see *a* change; but, it wasn't *the* change. Just before he sailed for home in July, 1867, he followed George Stuart's advice and attended the General Assembly in Edinburgh, "and it did me a world of good."[3]

But, all of these things together were not enough!

*   *   *

In early 1869, the unhappy young Apollos found Aquila and Priscilla in his own congregation,[4] "two elderly, Free Methodist women in frail health," Mrs.

[2]John Macpherson, *Henry Moorhouse, the English Evangelist.*

[3]*New York Tribune,* "Glad Tidings" (Report Hippodrome Meetings, 1876).

[4]This date is definitely fixed by Jessie McKinnon.

Cooke and Mrs. Snow. During the noon prayer-meetings in Farwell Hall, they made him nervous just the way they looked at him. He knew he was deficient somewhere; and he knew *they* knew it, too.

The sum of their estimate of him came out in several flying conversations at the end of the meetings: "They were *praying* for him. They saw he wasn't in the will of God; not filled with the Spirit; they were praying for *him!*" Just as if he were a sinner! Why, that got completely under his skin. "He who had the largest congregation in Chicago; and there were so many conversions! Could anybody be *doing* more for God than he? No! a thousand times, No!" But his spirit found no help in this auto-bromide. He miserably knew something was wrong. He was belligerent toward those dreadful women when they were present; and miserably lonely when they didn't come.

*   *   *

By 1871, everything *seemed* to be moving on with much encouragement. That new associate with the golden voice, Ira D. Sankey, whom he had found at the Indianapolis Y. M. C. A. Convention of 1870, was just packing them in at the new church building on Illinois Street. And no pastor could be surer of the love of his people—there was that magnificent new home which they had presented to Emma and himself. And there was his wonderful, new Farwell Hall which had become a Chamber of Commerce talking point.

Nevertheless, a mauling depression seized his soul. His little prayer-closet where he spent the time each day from 11.00 to 11.40 a.m. just before the great noon service, became a place of tears-"Oh God what's wrong with me?"

*   *   *

In April, 1871, the wooden coach train of the Overland Union-Southern Pacific curved its way east-bound through the Western deserts. Moody had secretly rejoiced in this opportunity to get away from his burden in Chicago, accompanying John H. Vincent and the singer, Philip Phillips, to the California State Sunday School Convention. But he hadn't escaped. He suddenly felt "terribly alone." Summer was coming on, and he hated to face his task in Chicago. His congregations had shown signs of falling away. Then, in long hours on the pioneer transcontinental, he felt his soul drop into the deepest pit awaiting flesh workers; "The gospel would not draw-*by itself.* He'd have to resort to some kind of sacred concerts, or get some one to lecture to get his crowds back again."[5] His like-minded brethren in 1936 are the over-wrought chaps who spend miserable hours in "the religious services" they arrange, where the gospel is supplemented by Hollywood films; and then go home thanking God it's over for another week.

He became so agitated that he could no longer sit with Vincent and Phillips. On the little open, rear coach platform, he felt a deep sense of shame. His

[5]Verbatim quotation, Washburne Collection.

compromise thinking was like a dog returning to its vomit. The gospel *wasn't* weak. *He* knew better than that after consorting with Spurgeon and Müller and Moorhouse. . . "Oh God have mercy! There is something wrong with *me!* In His dear Name, correct me! I'd rather die than go on this way." He covered his face, and Spring deserts slipped by unheeded.

XI
TILL A HOLY ONE GIVES HIM AN ACCOLADE OF FIRE
(November, 1871)

"I do not know of anything that America needs more today than men and women on fire with the fire of heaven; and I have yet to find a man or woman on fire with the Spirit of God that is a failure. I believe it is utterly impossible. They are never discouraged or disheartened. They rise higher and higher and it grows better and better all the while. My dear friends, if you haven't this illumination, make up your mind you are going to have it. Pray "O God, illuminate me with Thy Holy Spirit!"–D. L. *Short Talks*, Colportage Library, page 100.

"I was in the church ten years before I knew anything especially about the Holy Spirit. When I heard a man in a noon meeting say that the Spirit was a person, I thought he was gone daft. It is dreadful to see the powerless efforts of men trying to do a spiritual work without spiritual power. . . . Men are turned against the gospel by workers without the energy and wisdom of the Holy Spirit. . . And, the Holy Spirit coming upon men with power is distinct and separate from conversion. I would rather go to breaking stones in the road than to go into Christian work without the anointing of the Holy Spirit."–Hartzler, *Moody in Chicago.*

TILL A HOLY ONE GIVES HIM AN ACCOLADE OF FIRE
(November, 1871)

The preeminent blessing of a centennial study of Moody is reserved for all earnest hearts, troubled over a fruitless Christian life, that are praying, "Oh God, illuminate *me*. How may *I* find the hidings of power?" Here is a divine apologetic, proving that the most vigorous Christian falls miserably short, "if his labors are not in the Spirit." Had Moody died in his thirty-fourth year, on the train journey, his story would present no values worth toiling to observe. Let the Holy One be our Nathan, bluntly telling us as we grieve over the miserable Marathon Dominie of Illinois Street, "*Thou* art the man!" And then, when we watch him, utterly crushed, painfully tearing down lifetime habits of human thinking, substituting Written Wisdom, come on a sudden to an amazing gate that opened right into Third Heaven, let each burdened one weep with joy, "This may be *my* life story, too!" It cannot be otherwise than that a host of us, who in this age have surrendered to a cellophane ministry, delicately questing anywhere or everywhere for truth–save in God's Revelation–will suddenly receive *the* Fire that brings music at midnight, opens prison doors, and turns a hirdy-girdy age upside down.

*　　*　　*

Many a man has gone down into his Arabia with God during the hours of a long train journey. After a while, on that early Golden State Limited, Moody's tears gave way to solid introspection. The past three years rose up for review like Scrooge's ghosts. He remembered young Moorhouse saying to him in 1867, "You are sailing on the wrong tack. If you will change your course, and learn to preach *God's words* instead of your own, He will make you a great power." Then he saw himself immediately tumble into the Brea Pits of Scholastic Psychology–a hot haste to explain what the Bible *teaches* before dyeing his soul with what it *says*. Providentially the *course of reading* which a learned Chicago friend had suggested, together with the list of books, had been lost.

He could hear Moorhouse's rejoinder as to *a course of reading*, "You need only *one* Book for the study of the Bible!" Then he remembered his own nettled answer, "Moorhouse, you must have studied *many* books to come by your knowledge of the Bible"; and, Moorhouse's baffling reply, "I am a man of *one* Book. If a text of Scripture troubles me, I ask another text to explain it; if this will not answer I carry it straight to the Lord." Then he wept again, on the train platform, as he recalled his poignantly sweet joy when Moorhouse gave a private demonstration of "Bible Reading" for sixty people in Moody's home.

The Spirit gave him no rest. He saw he had been ambitious, not preaching for Christ, really; he "was preaching for ambition; he found everything in his heart that ought not to be there." He remembered with new understanding what an old man had said to him away back in Boston, in 1857, after Moody had spoken in Sunday school, "Young man, when you speak again, honor the Holy Ghost." He saw also that after Moorhouse left Chicago, he didn't follow the new light, but *took a course of reading.* And when he preached, he did as the Sons of Impotence have always done. He didn't honor the Holy Spirit; he took a text and departed from it! As a minister charged before God and the Lord Jesus Christ to preach the Word, he had clung to maxim preaching and had never tried the Word.

Then in the desert loneliness of that hour, he made a great decision: When he got back to Chicago, he'd launch out on *Bible* preaching, however much he'd stumble. A large part of a morning had passed when he, with smoke-blackened features, rejoined Vincent and Phillips. But a strange little song was in his heart. They laughed at his grimy face and said, "You must have enjoyed it!" And he cryptically rejoined, "It was wonderful!"

*   *   *

This new decision was much confirmed when he observed the powerful effect of William Morley Function's sermon on Daniel, delivered in Farwell Hall in May, even if it was "in awful orotund." He began to study the Bible on his knees. A breath from the Hills of Myrrh immediately came into his sermons. Strangely, he utterly stopped urging people to begin the Christian life by finding something to *do* for Christ; he now said, "Let Christ do something for *you!* Something for nothing!" At the close of a June service, one of the Dreadful Women put her hand lightly on his arm. Ordinarily, he wouldn't have stood for that. People couldn't paw over him! Especially, women! But he waited with trembling heart; and she said, "Lad, Jehovah is dealing with thee!"

He just couldn't keep back the tears. After all, these Dreadful Women had so much of the gentleness of Christ. His pride went smashing down. "Oh," he stammered, "Won't you please come to my house and talk to me?" Then followed a visit, the first of several, in which Ananias did mighty Paul instruct.

These mothers in Israel were all love and gentleness. They knew he was *sincere.* They knew he was *unselfish.* They *loved* him for it. But, that wasn't enough. He was still far from Eye-Guidance; his will was still carnal. "And at no place is man's un-Illumined will more dangerous than when it serves the altar." They prayed for him. He was humbled to the dust. After they left, he came back into the parlor, and covered his face with his hands. Then he felt Emma's sweet touch on his shoulder and heard her say, "Dearest, they're right!"

The superhot summer of 1871 blazed down in June. Well, he wouldn't worry about congregations; he'd just put God to the test, and though he did a poor job of it, he'd preach the Word. At first he sensed his dreadful ignorance. Then, he made the rewarding committal of giving even his ignorance to Christ. He began a series on Bible characters; Abraham, and Moses, and Daniel, and Paul, and Samuel, and David, and John, one after another. (See Colportage Library.)

With chastened heart, he observed how the Word was honored. New life flooded the Illinois Street Church. Sankey was like an angel. Even sweltering August didn't abate the attendance. In a spirit of rejoicing he began, in September, a new series of sermons on the life of Christ. More than three thousand people jammed Farwell Hall Sunday night, October 8. Power was there! Ten people raised hands for prayer before final exhortation began. Sankey was singing,

> "Today the Saviour calls:
> For refuge fly;
> The storm of justice falls,
> And death is nigh,"——

Suddenly, there was a wild alarm of fire, followed by the noise of fire-engines rushing past the hall; the tolling of bells, with ever and anon the deep sullen tones of the great city bell in the steeple of the old court-house close at hand. It was a general alarm! Sankey's voice was drowned out; the audience became restless and alarmed, and Moody abruptly closed the meeting—for which he never forgave himself.

The Moodys and the Sankeys went out a back stairway of Farwell Hall, and for a while watched the reflection of the roaring fire half a mile west.[1]

[1] Sankey's remarkable account in *My Life.*

Moody said, "This means ruin to Chicago." In a few minutes the Sankeys went over the river to where the fire was raging, and the Moodys went to their home on the north side. And they did not meet again until nearly Christmas!

It is pointless here to review the great Chicago fire that raged from Sunday night, October 8, to Wednesday, October 11. . . To envision the flames, fanned by a southwest wind, gripping whole blocks of frame buildings, . . the flying embers at night, . . the steady spread toward city center, . . the explosion of dynamite as General Sheridan blew down buildings to form fire barriers, . . the white faced terror of the homeless people, . . the fire-glow seen for hundreds of miles over the prairie and lake. . .

The next time you are in Chicago, go to the Chicago Historical Society, and operate their dramatic little diorama; see for yourself. When the fire burned out, 2,100 acres were burned over, 17,450 buildings were destroyed, running to a property damage of one hundred and ninety-two millions; two hundred and fifty people were killed, and one hundred and fifty thousand made homeless.[2] And among other tragic heaps, were the smoking ruins of Moody's new home, the new church building on Illinois Street, and the new Farwell Hall.

This was surely a year of heavy chastening to him. But it left him in a curious frame of mind. Somehow his trust in God had so deepened that he counted

[2]Statistics, Courtesy Chicago Historical Society.

it all joy. He never was so unhappy about *himself*; and never so rapturously satisfied with his Saviour. So, he would trust God! He could sincerely tell people after the fire that "he had much more left than he had lost."[3] Now what was to be done? Being criticized for a too generous distribution of help among the refugees, he decided to take his family east for a time, at least; and to find some sort of work there. At any rate, he could be raising funds to build a new, temporary church building.

*   *   *

In Brooklyn he visited a little mission chapel recently dedicated, a part of Theodore Cuyler's out-station work. The clean smell of new wood, paint, carpets, brought a rush of tears as he remembered his own beloved buildings. "It seemed full of heaven. If only he could hold a meeting there." The remark was repeated to Doctor Cuyler, and an instant invitation resulted.

But, it was again the *old* Moody who preached, the sawdust topic-taker! Why did he take that sterile course, especially after what he had learned? Maybe it was because the devil had saved a few "pet sermons" out of the holocaust. Formerly they were always sure-fire; now, he saw they were ashes. The congregations swiftly dropped to eighteen. There was another woman in the meetings with the same terrible meekness of the Chicago pair. He trembled one night at service-end when she said:

[3] *Pleasure and Profit in Bible Study*, p. 96.

"We have plenty of *preaching* in Brooklyn; but if you will *tell us something about the Bible* it will be blessed to us."

He wept in his room to think what a fool he had been, always letting his eyes run toward the pagan hills for help, forgetting *his* help should come from the Lord. "God forgive him! and help him"—to "go simple again." The next afternoon, it was not an early sermonic peacock that he preened for a restrutting, but a simple Bible reading. The ravishingly sweet Fires of God at once came down, enveloping not only the little mission, but sweeping right up into Cuyler's home church. So mighty a visitation was it, that a church in Philadelphia invited him to hold meetings there. When he arrived in Philadelphia the idea of using old, sure-fire sermons was repugnant. He had a heart for nothing now but the glory of the Word.

*   *   *

A strangely changed Moody walked down a New York street one night in November. He had never been drunk with wine in his life. But now, he knew the exultation which Satan's counterfeit imitated. Every time he stepped, one foot said "glory" and the other responded "hallelujah." Suddenly he sobbed, "Oh God, why don't you *compel* me to walk close to Thee, always? Deliver me from myself! Take absolute sway! Give me Thy Holy Spirit!"

And suddenly the little red room called his heart was filled as with a mighty rushing wind. . . He

couldn't bear the rapture of it. . . He had to be alone. . . .
He knew a friend near-by who had a room where he could
find refuge in this storm. . . There were hours following,
of which it was unlawful to speak, and he seldom did. But,
a triple battery of reporters caught him one day in New
York, four years later, as he spoke to several thousand
ministers and laymen, and it is my good fortune to have
had their report put into my hands.[4]

"He felt constrained against all his habits to
communicate a personal experience. The fruits of
his preaching had been small and few. In distress he
walked the streets of the great city by night—'Oh
God, anoint me with Thy Spirit!' . . God heard him
. . . and gave him right on the street what he had
begged for. . . Words could not express the
Influence upon him. . . He had been trying to *pump*
water out of a well that seemed dry. . . He pumped
with all his might and little water came. . . Then
God had made his soul like an *Artesian* well that
could never fail of water. . .He knew now what a
Lovely Someone meant when He said, 'But the
water that I shall give him shall be in him a well of
water springing up into everlasting life!'"

*   *   *

George H. Stuart and John Wanamaker seemed
mysteriously led to put into Moody's hands $3,000,
just enough to go ahead and build a temporary struc-

[4]Copy furnished through kindness of O. C. Colton, La Mesa, Calif.

ture on the lot the brethren back in Chicago had secured, corner of Wells and Ontario Streets. Acting on his telegraphic orders, they built the North Side Tabernacle, where the church was to worship in a desert of ashes for three years.

The edifice was a rambling, barnlike structure, one hundred and nine feet long, seventy-five wide, built of rough-sawn timbers and boards, lined with heavy paper to keep out the cold; it's tar and gravel flattop being supported with lines of beams and posts, "like a stable." Much of the work was done by people who lived in wretched hovels and holes in the sidewalk. And since the King had provided a new Moody, He also provided a new Sankey; a changed musician who arose somehow out of the mystery of Chicago's ashes. When the building was completed, the people wired their pastor to come home for the dedication.

Moody looked over the vast crowd in the rambling building on the evening of December 24, 1871. Where in the world did they come from? More than a thousand children, accompanied by their parents! Many sobbed with joy as he "opened the Book." He suddenly became aware that directly in front of him were those two Dreadful—no! No! a thousand times, No! those two *Angels of Light!* It just seemed that made his joy complete, that *they* were there!

Heaven had certainly touched earth during that two hours dedication. He stood, after service, meeting friends. And here at last were those two *Wonderful* Women. There was such an expression in their faces as they looked at him that he "wanted to fall at the feet of Jesus in thanksgiving." And now they are saying something to him—words sweeter to hear as coming from them than from anyone else in all the world:

> "And after the fire a Still Small Voice! Now, walk softly, Lad, all the days of thy life! *Jehovah hath dealt with thee!*"

XII
THE HOLY ONE GREATLY ENRICHES HIS PANOPLY
(December, 1871–June, 1873)

If the Most Excellent Theophilus of Centennial Year is determined to know *experimentally*, the certainty of those things recorded in the Romance of Faith, he is again admonished to regard the Sequence of Heaven. No reason appears for expecting any change in the lovely processional of blade, ear and, after that, full corn in the ear. The more carefully we regard how Moody's life was caused to grow heavenward "from above," (anothen); and the more accurately our understanding becomes closely traced (parakolouthekoti), the more importance we attach to the very *order* of events.

There are only a few lines on this Shadow Page. To every Don Quixote, who zealously scans horizons for the Wind Mills of Hair Splitting,-well, he can quickly upset this little chap,-and ride on. But, today's Chieftains of Judah, praying to be made as a pan of fire among wood, will find that those who make a discriminating study of the *order* of Moody's unfolding, shall have their reward.-*Sketch Book.*

The Holy One Greatly Enriches His Panoply
(December, 1871-June, 1873)

For many years, the Varley slogan has been the major premise for conclusions that have simply failed to work:

> "Consecrate yourselves perfectly to God, and *then* you shall have power. Look at Moody! One time when he was young he heard somebody say that, 'It has yet to be seen, etc., etc.' He decided to be that man himself, and see what he did!"

Thousands have earnestly tried it, suffered muddy frustration, and then with Artaban have signed off with, "This quest is not for me!"

As a matter of simple chronology, Moody's life reveals that *first* he received power, and *afterward*, exhibited consecration! It is neither historically nor scripturally true that, "Whenever there is abandonment to the will of God, there is an enduement of the power of God." But the reverse is divinely accurate, "Whenever there is an enduement of the power of God, *then* there is abandonment to the will of God." Not important? Well, it is singular that an Ancient Record insists with Cosmic Fire that it is *first*, Power, then witnessing; not, witnessing, then power (Acts 1:8).

The Varley slogan came into Moody's life comparatively late, in July, 1872. He was then over thirty-five! And, it came *after* that New York November night!

*   *   *

Moody and Sankey lived in the draughty North Side Tabernacle during the winter of 1871-1872, "They were as poor as the people around them," but they were so filled with hope and happiness that, though poor, they were able to make many rich, having nothing but possessing all things.

The building was kept warm day and night; wave after wave of revival swept the people; "almost a continual service for months together, crowds weeping over sin one day, shouting over pardon the next; dispirited men and women seemed to absorb Moody's overflowing gladness." Relief activities of colossal proportions went on day after day, but always under this dominant ideal, "What is the use of keeping these poor people's bodies a little longer out of the grave and not trying to keep their souls out of hell?" (D. L.'s own statement.)

How the glory of God came down upon the rude wooden building! It was the one bright spot in the shadowed lives of men, women, and children, who walked for miles through the snowy ruins, just to see and to hear Moody and Sankey and Emma Dryer! Just at this point, the top-grace enduement of 1 Peter 4:8 came upon the Church in full power: "Above all things *being fervent in your* love among yourselves!"

If one misses the *love* note in the Chicago Moody institutions, he will remain baffled by their perennial vitality. One desperately cold day in the winter of 1933, I made my way through a blizzard to the Moody Church, and would have had no surprise to see a half-empty auditorium. But when I opened the door, thousands were already seated; thousands whose spirits were moving in a world of ever-blooming flowers, while winter snarled outside. . . One disgustingly hot July morning, 1935, I went to the Bible Institute. The vigorous hundreds in that big bee-hive seemed to have no particular annoyance at the muggy temperatures that make westerners hum, "California, Here I Come!" They had forgotten that May and June were torn off the calendar. And the underlying reason for this perennial vitality is that, beginning with a Kern River onsweep in the sixties, their "love for the brethren" has expanded into an ocean.

Moody's first vision of "the greatest thing in the world" came to him during the Moorhouse meetings in 1867. (Remember Drummond *got* this *from* Moody; he didn't *give* it *to* him.) For a solid week, Moorhouse preached upon John 3:16. Moody said:

> "I never knew up to that time that God loved us so much. This heart of mine began to thaw out; I could not keep back the tears. I just drank it in. So did the crowded congregation. I tell you there is one thing that draws above everything else in the world and that is love."

He saw then, in 1867, for the first time, the secret of a winsome church:

> "The churches would soon be filled if outsiders could find that people in them loved them when they came. This draws sinners! We must win them to us first, then we can win them to Christ. We must get the people to love us, and then turn them over to Christ."

But it is one thing to know that love is the conquering weapon; quite another to secure it. Moorhouse blessed Moody still further by showing him that love comes from first finding but exactly what the Bible *says*, not what it *teaches*.

> "I took up that word 'Love,' and I do not know how many weeks I spent in studying the passages 'in which it occurs, *till at last I could not help loving people!* (Italics mine.) I had been feeding on Love so long that I was anxious to do everybody good I came in contact with."[1]

> "I got full of it. It ran out my fingers. *You* take up the subject of love *in the Bible!* You will get so full of it that all you have got to do is to open your lips, and a flood of the Love of God flows out upon the meeting. There is no use trying to do church work without love. A doctor, a lawyer, may do good work without love, but God's work cannot be done without love."

[1] D. L. M., *Pleasure and Profit in Bible Study.*

This had all the romance of new-world discovery for Moody; and his church was greatly blessed. But he did not feel *apostolic* love come over his church until after his own accolade.

> "How could he? One couldn't have the fullest *fruits* of the Spirit without first fully having the Spirit. And the very first fruit of the Spirit was love. Therefore, let every Christian make up his mind he's going to have the Spirit. Pray 'Oh God, give me the Spirit.' After he had received the Spirit he went to preaching again. He had no new truth to present, yet hundreds were converted. Church love waxed into a June glory."

In 1872, Moody issued an appeal for funds to build a permanent edifice; the North Side Tabernacle could no longer be endured. By October, the lot, corner of Chicago Avenue and La Salle Street, was purchased, and the work of constructing the edifice of the Chicago Avenue Church begun.

Records show that about five hundred thousand Sunday school children furnished their mites in response to the slogan, "five cents a brick." The building, seating 2,000, was of brick and stone, "in dreadful Gothic." (You may see it in the Moody Bible Institute picture, page 250, lower left-hand corner). The depression of 1872-1873, and the strict carrying out of Moody's rule "No debt; no further than the funds!" caused the construction to "halt at the second floor, and be roofed over." On July 16, 1873, when D. L. was in his English revival, the one story was dedicated free of debt, total cost of building and land being $89,000. In 1876, it was entirely finished by hymn-book royalties, and continued as a flaming center of evangelism, until in 1915, its vigorous daughter, the Moody Bible Institute, took it over entirely, and the church moved to a new location, at North Avenue, Clarke and La Salle Streets. There they erected a temporary wooden tabernacle, seating five thousand. The history of the institution, now renamed "The Moody Memorial Church," is resumed in Chapter XX.

*   *   *

In 1872, Moody felt guided to make his second English visit. This short trip, from late June to September—"Without Emma, Sankey being in charge of the Tabernacle"—was the culminating factor in preparing him for the world-wide revival movement. Three great things came of it: A Spirit-filled man received enlightenment as to the boundless possibilities of complete surrender; "he saw England was ready," and a certain few in England saw that "Moody was ready for it."

His chief purpose in this second visit was to further increase his Bible knowledge, which he hoped to do in the Dublin Mildmay Conference. "He had no intention to teach; he went as a learner." But on his way to the conference, he consented to supply the pulpit of John Lessey, in North London. This was the occasion of the much-told story, "No particular interest in the morning; power of God at night; Moody's return in a few days; a mighty revival; four hundred converted; discovery that an invalid, elderly lady had prayed the revival down!" Now, in no way is the power of intercessory prayer deprecated when we say, that story has been distressingly "wrested." Just as if that dear old Christian lady were *responsible* for the revival! Moody himself never said so. Look it up. He *did* regard it as illustrating the *value* of prayer. But, *the real reason* for that revival was that D. L. Moody was now *the* "Burning Bush"; his humble, human nature so filled with Fire that the world was beginning to turn aside to see. Only one more work of grace remained to be done upon him, of which we are now about to speak. Then, the candle being Flame-tipped, God set it in a stick appropriate to its power.

Arriving in Dublin, Moody joined for three days with the Plymouth Brethren in the Mildmay Conference, the chief session being held in Merrion Hall. He, and others, were entertained on the estate of Henry Bewley, a sturdy old Calvinist, and "the pocket-book of the Dublin Tract Society."

One of Bewley's guests was Henry Varley.

It is due to Varley, just as it is due to Ira David Sankey, that we bring him out of the shadows, and know him better. Two years Moody's senior, he was born in 1835. His mother was a woman of unusual culture, a seminary president. But Varley, owing to her early death, missed formal education. At twelve he joined a Baptist Church, "received a work of grace at fifteen," and at nineteen (1854) went to Australia as a "Gospel-preaching gold-digger." Returned to England in 1857. (Yes, it was

the lovely girl who became Mrs. Varley.) He purchased a
large meat business (hence "Butcher Varley") and as a
side-line engaged in lay preaching.

So powerfully did God witness to him that while still a
big-scale business man, he built a many-galleried church
which up to 1900 was called the West London
Tabernacle, St. James. There he served as a "pastor" for
twenty years. He was always a welcome speaker in
Spurgeon's church. He and Henry Moorhouse were
"inseparable." He left a trail of evangelism all over the
world, making ten trips to Australia, three to America,
two to Canada, and side apostolates into South Africa,
India, Siam. Ah, there were giants in those days!

During the Dublin conference, the guests of good old
Henry Bewley gathered early one morning in a large
haymow "for a season of special prayer, confession and
renewed consecration." Grattan Guiness and Henry
Varley were present. (Remember, Varley was then in full
stride, thirty-seven years old.) In a quiet way, and in deep
humility, at a hushed interval in this haymow conference,
Varley said (and he spoke out of his own living
experience),

"THE WORLD HAS YET TO SEE WHAT GOD CAN DO
WITH AND FOR AND THROUGH AND IN A MAN WHO
IS FULLY AND WHOLLY CONSECRATED TO HIM."

This chance remark greatly moved Moody; one
can sense how profoundly, in remembering that
Moody looked Varley up in June, 1873, (right after

he returned to England, at the beginning of the Great Awakening) and said, "Oh, brother! those were the words of the Lord through your lips to my soul!"

When he returned to London two days later to preach in Lessey's church, he slipped into Spurgeon's Tabernacle and went to the same high gallery seat he occupied in 1867. Heaven again "came down on his soul." Spurgeon looked like an angel to him. While he listened to Spurgeon he could hear young Varley's statement over and over:

> "'The world had yet to see! with and for and through and in! A man!' Varley meant *any* man! Varley didn't say he had to be educated, or brilliant, or anything else! Just, *a man!* Well, by the Holy Spirit in him, he'd be *one* of those men. And then suddenly, in that high gallery, he saw something he'd never realized before,–it was not Mr. Spurgeon, after all, who was doing that work: it was God. And if God could use Mr. Spurgeon, why should He not use the rest of us, and why should we not all just lay ourselves at the Master's feet, and say to Him, 'Send me! use me!'"[2]

People in the balcony that day noted a stocky young fellow who wept a great deal; but who stoutly insisted it was not a matter of sin or penitence; it was Third Heaven glory. He had just found some-

[2]The above narrative is not semi-fiction, but is in Moody's own words. See *Autobiography, Spurgeon,* Judson Press, Vol. IV, pages 246-248.

thing out, something very wonderful to him. And he was so happy, he just couldn't help himself.

*   *   *

He proceeded with the meeting at Lessey's church. As the power of God came down, he prayed, "Dear Master, don't you think I could be used to stir England for Thee?" Almost instantly an answer came to this prayer. Good old Henry Bewley, Rev. William Pennyfather, rector of St. Judes, Mildmay Park, London, and Mr. Cuthbert Bainbridge, of New-Castle-on-Tyne, formally invited him to hold meetings in England:

> "They felt the power of God was on Mr. Moody, and a blessing would come to England if he would go back to Chicago, fix up his work, and return at once for a series of meetings. They would guarantee the salary of any helper he might bring. And they would advance necessary traveling expenses. Would Mr. Moody do it?"

"Would Mr. Moody do it!" He couldn't think of anything he desired so much to do. How slowly the vessel returned toward New York! He wanted to tell Emma the good news! And Sankey! They would all go to England! Immediately! Together! And that was that!

(Note to the Gentle Reader: The dramatic sequence is suspended at this point, and resumed in Chapter XV. The next two chapters, which constitute a vignette biography of Sankey, are in reality a parallel account. It will be found helpful, in thinking of the great revival beginning 1873, to be acquainted with Sankey's contribution, and to orientate it to the resumption of the narrative, which begins again in the chapter, "The World Turns Aside.")

PILGRIM AND THE MAN WITH THE MELODEON

(Washburne Collection)

MOODY AND SANKEY
as they appeared at the beginning of the Great Revival, 1873

IRA DAVID SANKEY
Born August 28, 1840;   Died August 13, 1908

But now bring me a minstrel. And it came to pass when the minstrel
played, that the hand of the Lord came upon him."–2 Kings 3:15.

XIII
HE IS JOINED BY A MAN WITH A MELODEON
(August 28, 1840–June, 1873)

"It is a mistake to regard the sermon as the only important thing or even the main thing. There is often more gospel in gospel hymns than in the sermon. Song carries the gospel into many hearts the sermon does not reach."-D. L. M.

"Mr. Moody treats spiritual themes in a business-like way. . . . Hence the songs of Sankey, marked by a certain tenderness, come in to complement what is wanting in the speaker,-a fitting union of the two that makes the whole complete."-A Philadelphia newspaper editorial.

"Men untouched by anything Mr. Moody says, break down under the song-question, 'What Will the Harvest Be?' They go into the inquiry rooms. . . Song-words of Mr. Sankey, made sharp by the Spirit, account for his power."- An 1874 issue of "The Moravian."

"I'm glad to be only an armor-bearer for my beloved friend D. L.

"'Only an armor-bearer, now in the field, guarding a shining helmet, sword and shield, waiting to hear the thrilling battle-cry. Ready then to answer, Master, here am I! Surely my Captain may depend on me, though but an armor-bearer I may be.'"-Sankey applies Bliss' song to his own life.

HE IS JOINED BY A MAN WITH A MELODEON
(August 28, 1840-June, 1873)

There is a mountain in Northern California whose summit, observed from surrounding valleys, appears to be a purple unity, thrust up against a blue sky. But a great surprise awaits all who follow the rough trail to the top. There in the high silence they find what seemed to have been a single peak is really four-one larger, three lesser. We never forget this experience as in after years we look up toward St. Helena.

Nor is it otherwise with D. L. Moody. Centennial thinking is enriched when it considers that an important part of the Commoner's figure, uplifted on the sky-line of the past century, is the contributing excellencies of three others-Betsey Holton, Emma Charlotte Revell, and Ira David Sankey. This man with a baby organ is much too important to be scattered through the chapters, as others of the compassing cloud. He deserves the recognition of a separate treatment, even as The Berkshire Madonna, and The Faithful Christiana. Especially, since he, too, sets forth the prodigy of a *bush*, aglow with the Fire of God.

Before the flair for "re-thinking" entirely passes, there is one area where it *could be* highly profitable-the field of church music. If one has that healing sincerity which admits that the contemporary church has let go, and if he is possessed of the set face to find how she may take hold again, let him go in for a long meditation in the desert upon that entire subject. And the Life of Sankey would prove a suggestive hand-book for pointing up that meditation.

Almost at once, a candid judgment on the whole subject of church music forces us to admit that putting the premium upon *technical excellence* has been the casting away of the shield of Saul which has made Gilboa dry and rainless. Lovely indeed is Music when she has the heart of a handmaid; but when she is suffered to become a mistress, alas! Evangel drops to the level of an intimidated consort. We face in Sankey an anomaly which, to use a figure recently popular with the intelligentsia, "ought to stab us wide awake." Precisely as God exhibited His contempt for mere academic excellence by means of the Fiery Apostolate of unlettered Moody, so He likewise confirmed His canon "Not by might," when He made untrained Sankey the voice of One crying in the wilderness.

Now in the things we are saying, the chief point is this: the glory of Christian music is that moving of the Spirit upon the poet who writes, the composer who finds the melody, and the performer, who sings, and sings with the understanding also. (This goes for the accompanist, too. His quality lies not simply in cunning playing, but-in that the Lord is with him. 1 Samuel 16:18.) Church music simply fails to register in the zone of power, unless-it has Witness. Herein was an annoying fact that certain musical experts faced in Sankey's day. They bought his music in reams, but were baffled to find that "though sung by the *best* voices to the most artistic accompaniment, it just wouldn't sound as it did in the meetings."

What a mass of testimony there is to set forth the convictions of careful witnesses upon the value of *Spiritual* songs! David esteemed them *the secret of a fruitful earth.* (Psalm 67:5, 6.) Luther thus spoke of the Reformation: "Next to theology, I give the highest honor to music." Make a careful study of Wesley's influence, and one perceives that thousands who cared but little for his preaching were attracted by his stirring new songs. Singular! When religion is vital, music is, also. When faith declines, the music likewise becomes intolerable, "a ceremonial racket." I have had much glee over a pastel nuance recorded in Matthew 9: 23, "And when Jesus came into the ruler's house and saw the minstrels and the people—*making a noise!*" Moody, who couldn't sing a note, had a cunning discernment: "I will not have songs that have no doctrine in them; nor singers without the Holy Spirit."

* * *

Sankey's unique views and rules of church music make a capital foil for regarding his whole career. People who might esteem Sankey to be "just another musician," more temperamental than tempered, should know that he moved upon lines of solid common sense quite up to those of his chief. I venture to present his views under the form of an Associated

Press Radio Interview. Of course such an interview never took place. But it could have. Every statement herein assigned to Sankey is in his own words and sentiment, as garnered from the dusty memorabilia of yesterday.

"Mr. Sankey, how much of this great awakening is due to the music?"

"Now *that* question is difficult for me to answer. Mr. Moody, of course, moves in the power of God, and the music is able to come to what it is, because he is what he is. But, I want to be pardoned in saying that ministers do not make as much of music as they could. Singing has been an important part of worship in all ages. *It should be prayed for as much as the preaching.*"

"Why do you use that little melodeon in churches where they have big pipe-organs?"

"I have always admired the large, noble instrument. It has an important place. But, in congregational singing, it drowns out the voices, and people just sit and listen without singing. The little organ gives the singers the key-note only. A capella is the noblest type of singing. Mr. Spurgeon does not suffer any kind of an instrument,-and you should hear them sing in Metropolitan."

"We have heard you do not want non-Christians in your choirs, however good their voices."

"That's correct. The choirs in churches should consist of Christians and be directed by a Christian musician. And further, I don't feel any one is competent to lead church music who isn't sufficiently interested in God's work to attend Sunday School, and prayer-meetings. If such leaders are suffered, they never exercise a marked influence on the choir for good. The power of God is as necessary in singing as in preaching. Choir practices should begin and end with prayer."

"We note you rule out all choir specials that go under the heading of 'classical music.' Why?"

"Well, they have but little religion in them. They draw attention to the skill of the performer. Old familiar hymns and tunes should be used, and even now and then a Sunday School song, so that the children will feel a part has been made for them."

"What weakness do you see in conventional church music?"

"Well, the end of church music is to lead sinners to Jesus, to quicken devotion, and to glorify God. 'Conventional music' is performed by singers who think of glorifying *themselves*. They have but little sympathy for the minister; they rattle leaves of books, or show listless inattention; they sing expressly for musical effect, and nothing more,–except the pay they expect to receive."

"Choirs have been called 'storm centers' of the church. Why?"

"Well, they do not need to be. Four-fifths of the traditional trouble is because of ungodly people in choirs."

"You do not seem to have 'a man with a little stick' leading the choir. Why?"

"The flourishing is distracting. When we come to worship God the less display, the better. Whatever stick-flourishing is done should be done in practice."

"Your choirs are always marked by fine propriety. Is that accidental?"

"Not entirely. We talk it over in rehearsals and pray about it. Deportment of singers should be in keeping with the house of God. Choir conduct has much to do with the success of preaching. Whispering, talking out loud, writing notes, passing books, heads down reading something, and the like, distract terribly. Such deportment grieves the children of God. Furthermore when a person sings in the choir, he ought to stay there, not get up and go out, even to sit in the congregation."

"How about young people and children in the choir?"

"By all means. They sing more heartily than any one else. Have children's choirs."

"Thank you, Mr. Sankey. We'll broadcast that down to the Moody Centennial in 1937. They'll like it, we're sure."

*   *   *

Ira David Sankey was born on a farm near Edensburg, Pennsylvania, August 28, 1840. His musical training was entirely that of "The Log Fire Conservatory," where in the evening this family of Quaker State Methodists "joyfully sang the songs of Zion to a little parlor organ." You know the kind–a breast-high, black walnut box, fronted by jig-cut, wood-scroll facings; music-rack covered with green baize; black ebony stops, with circular ivory name-plates; and pedals overlayed with red Brussels carpet.

He was converted at twelve in the little country church. When he was seventeen, the family moved to New Castle. At once he took an active part in the "city church"–choir leader, class leader, Sunday School Superintendent. Then, Y. M. C. A. "president." During his term of enlistment in the Civil War, he organized "musical soldiers for camp prayer-meetings." After his term expired, he returned to New Castle, and resumed his church duties with greater zeal than ever. He married a young lady in his choir, Fannie V. Edwards, September 9, 1863. The stern norms of biography forbid any further notice of Miss Edwards than to say, *she was altogether worthy of Emma Charlotte Revell*. Three children were born to them, two in America, prior to the Great Awakening, and one in Scotland during that period.

After the war, Sankey was given a post in the Internal Revenue Department, where he served for ten years, "at fifteen hundred per," until-Moody changed his plans. But these ten years were strategic to his future. Because of his golden voice, he came to an interstate popularity, "learning by what he did, and remembering what he learned."

In June, 1870, he was a delegate to the International Y. M. C. A. convention, Indianapolis. He attended a six a.m. prayer-service because "Young Moody of Chicago was announced as the leader and he was most curious to see him." D. L. plainly showed annoyance during the meeting over the dull, stupid singing. Rev. Robert McMillan, seated next to Sankey, nudged him and said, "Get up and sing something!" Sankey arose, and without accompaniment began,

> "There is a fountain filled with blood,
> Drawn from Immanuel's veins!"

Moody looked at him startled, and then dropped his eyes into the familiar prayer-pose which millions, in years following, saw him take whenever Sankey sang. After meeting, Moody held Sankey's hand and with machine-gun rapidity, asked him about his private life; then with Moody abruptness told him: "I've been looking for you seven years: you'll have to give up your Civil Service: come to Chicago: you sing: I'll talk." The whole account reads today like a captivating story of brutal psychology. Sankey went to Chicago "to look it over for a week." And at the end of the fifth day "sent his commission to the Secretary of the Treasury!" Lo, in youth's divine folly, he, a family man, was dropping a meal ticket to begin a new life for which he had no formal training. But, he was ready. And D. L. had guaranteed him twelve hundred a year!

Ten months later, April, 1871, he left his family behind, and began with Moody in Chicago. In September, 1871, Fannie Sankey with her baby, took up residence in the Lake City. In October, the red terror of fire seemingly upset their devoted plans. Like the Moodys they lost everything-yet kept all! Within four days, they were back in New Castle, the future very uncertain. In November-no man has yet revealed aught save the date-Sankey received his own Accolade. By January, 1872, he and Moody were again united, and began their "Apostolate of Ashes." The chronicle of the blessings Sankey's voice brought to the stricken homes is a chapter in the Romance of Faith. When Moody went on his second English visit in the summer of 1872, Sankey was left in charge of the Church, assisted by Major Whittle, Richard Thain, and Fleming H. Revell (II).

He warmed to Moody's plan that both families should go to England for an evangelistic campaign, "all expenses paid." But the dreary months of utter silence following, when no word was heard from the English Committee, was disheartening. Phillip Phillips approached him in May, 1873, with "golden inducements," to break with Moody and go on a concert tour of California. But Sankey was impelled to remain with Moody by reason of a glorious experience that came to him as he was "singing a song of Jesus to a child, dying in a shack among those dreadful ruins."

*   *   *

On June 7, 1873, the two stout young gentlemen sailed away to England to begin their special meetings. Sankey's two children were left behind with their grandparents; his loved Fannie went with him; and her fingers were busy with baby things.

His professional equipment was a Bagster's Bible, and "A seed plot," the name he gave to his musical scrap-book in which he had pasted his favorite songs for ten years. Conspicuous in his luggage was a comical little melodeon, which the disapproving Scotchmen called "A deil's kist o' whustles." Yes, it had to be put right on deck where every one could see it.

Let's have a look at this singer; the Washburne photos help. He was heavy, a trifle taller than Moody, but much ahead of him in personal grace. Both of them had brown eyes and brown beards. England was soon to find that besides his voice, Sankey had power as life changer; his thirty-three years of blameless life helped here. Gypsy Smith frequently narrates, with tears, how "young Sankey put his hand on my head, when I was a boy in Epping Forest and said, 'May the Lord make a preacher of you, my boy.'"

But that golden voice! Ah, here the yellowed records of yesterday grasp for adjectives.

"A strange quality that melted audiences into tears: every tone touched the heart. A voice so gentle it was never offensive. . . Yet so penetrating that an avowed atheist, sitting on his front porch, fuming because his family had gone to the Moody-Sankey meetings, heard Sankey in the Northfield Church *a mile away* singing the Ninety and Nine,-and was converted! . . A hush came over the listening thousands as if they had been brushed by angels' wings. . . When he finished singing the death-like silence was broken by sobs and leaf rattling like a storm . . . just one way to describe it, when he sang, he became transparent, and Jesus stood just behind him . . . hundreds would silently gather below his open hotel window just to hear him practice! . . he always selected his songs by Guidance . . . he seemed to paint pictures in music . . . and what he sang mysteriously clinched what Moody preached."

*   *   *

It seemed incredible that this odd pair, evangelist and singer, was in three months to walk into the very center of British attention. Canny Dr. John Kelman, pastor in Edinburg's suburb, Leith, attended the Newcastle-on-Tyne meeting incognito. ("He wore an old soft white hat instead of his high silk topper.") As a result, Moody and Sankey were invited to Edinburg. Both of the young men had serious misgivings. The former feared, "What can such as I do among those Scotch divines?" The latter knew his little organ was nefast to Scotch Christians. For three hundred years organs were forbidden in the churches. Andrew Bonar, anxious to be conciliatory, assured the fretting Presbyterians that the organ "was a very *little* one."

And Sankey feared also concerning his "human hymns." Moody "tactfully" tried to clear the way by admonishing the Scotchmen, "Don't forget, brethren, that the Psalms were written under the Old Dispensation!" Herein, however, lay the divine corrective. It was inevitable that Psalms should eventually give way to hymns. Christians really wanted the Living Christ of the New Testament, rather than His shadow in the Old.

With such apprehensions, there was nought for them to do but to walk into their Scottish mission by faith, and faith alone. Lo, it stirs one's heart to behold them, utterly unconscious that the approval of heaven was just about to fall.

XIV
AND THE CHURCH BEGINS TO SING!
(July, 1873–August 13, 1908)

"I do not know how we shall stand the first day in heaven. Do you not think we shall break down in the songs from over delight? I once gave out the hymn,

> 'There is a land of pure delight
> Where saints immortal dwell.'

An aged man standing in front of the pulpit sang heartily the first verse, and then sat down weeping. I said to him afterwards, 'Father Linton, what made you cry over that hymn?' He said, 'I could not stand it,-the joys that are coming!'"-*Talmadge*.

. . . .

But first century preaching and first century music must reappear together. If the sermons, anemic because Bloodless, are made to consort with true gospel singing, there is an incongruity sadly limiting the hymns, and they appear *cheap*. If a fervid herald of evangelical truth is supported by Coué Choirs-you know, "Let us hasten! Let us hasten! Let us hasten-to the tomb!" . . Well, then the music sounds *stupid*. But when in the grace of God they arrive already paired, ah, then one senses what good old Richard Baxter felt,-"I had the liveliest foretaste of heaven on earth; and I could almost wish that our voices were loud enough to reach through the world, and to heaven itself!"-*Sketch Book*.

AND THE CHURCH BEGINS TO SING
(July, 1873-August 13, 1908)

The party arrived in Edinburg during a stretch of dismal Scotch weather. The first service was scheduled for Sunday, November 23, 1873. And tragically, in such a dilemma, Sankey had to "go it alone"-Moody had a severe cold.

An hour before the service started, the building was packed. Sankey said: "I tell you it was a trying time; Moody absent; there I was alone, with my 'human hymns' and 'kist o' whustles'!" But before the service was finished "the intense silence over the big crowd, and the suspiciously moist eyes, proved that Scotland *might* receive these musical innovations *if they came in the Spirit.*" When in closing Sankey fearfully suggested that they join him in the chorus of Bliss' "Hold the Fort," it sounded like the clans a'gangin' to war!

At the second meeting Moody had to "go it alone." The "kist o' whustles" got badly messed up when a Jehu expressman turned his cart over while rounding a corner, and dumped the *thing* upon the cobbles.

In the third meeting both Moody and Sankey were able to take part. Dr. Horatius Bonar, particularly feared by Sankey, sat close to the melodeon. Sankey prayed, "Oh God, help me!" and began to play with no small fear. But the glory of the Lord immediately filled the tabernacle and so abode for two hours. At the end, Sankey again asked God to bless him, ran his fingers over the little keyboard and sang,

> Once for all, oh, sinner receive it!
> Once for all, oh, brother believe it!
> Cling to the cross, the burden will fall,
> Christ hath redeemed us once for all.

Doctor Bonar moved rapidly over to Sankey, seized his hand, and, "Mon, Mon! but ye *did* sing the gospel tonight!"

From there on Bonny Scotland opened her heart to the American cousins-and they let the little organ in, too. In three months the whole nation was singing-on the streets, in the shipyards, on the trains, in the market-places. In a few months more the churches of all Christendom took up the refrains. By 1876, the angels were listening to an international choir.

"It was easy and blessed and natural, then, (to use a cherished phrase of my friend from Dallas) to do Christian work." Joyful singing arose out of faithful preaching; and heart-doors were opened to the ministers' messages by the glory of spiritual music. One couldn't tell for the life of him which depended on the other,

> Sie fragen es nicht,
> Sie wissen im Herzen
> Dass die beide
> Für einander sind!¹

America was already familiar with the Sankey songs when the Brooklyn revival began, October

---

¹They don't even question; they know in their hearts that the two of them are each for the other.

24, 1875. Some feared this would dull the interest. Did it? "No! a thousand times, No!" America vied with Great Britain, so that, go where you would, from Frosty Calais to Sunny San Diego, city men, farm-hands, and cowboys were singing,

> Dare to be a Daniel,
>> Dare to stand alone,
> Dare to have a purpose firm,
>> And dare to make it known!

And now after sixty years there is a mystic release whenever these songs are sung in the churches. Try them out. Lo, one quickly finds that they have that beaten oil whereby the lamp doth burn continually. Sometimes the sweet singers of Zion come singly; sometimes they appear in constellations like stars. Such was the case in the day of Moody and Sankey, the latter half of the nineteenth century. Whosoever takes it upon himself to provide another book for the Moody Centennial, under such a title as *The Songs of a World Awakening,* will surely do goodness unto Israel. The minstrels and their music, too numerous for more than a swift inventory, could therein be studied in detail; such names as McGranahan, Sweeney, Root, Towner, Stout, Kirkpatrick, Main, Stebbins, Excell, Doane-time fails me.

Let us regard briefly some of these men and their music. A fair number of songs, composed prior to 1873, had been pasted in Sankey's scrap-book before he sailed for England. Others, appearing from time to time, were added. This gave him a growing repertoire, the music upon which he depended. In the early part of this period, up to the year 1880, a tidy little group of the dependables were of Sankey's own composition. It was not until he began in Scotland, in 1873, that he attempted hymn composition, but after that he composed the music to Miss Clephane's "The Ninety and Nine," and "Beneath the Cross of Jesus";[2] the melody for the anonymous poem "Go Bury Thy Sorrow"; Stites' "Trusting Jesus that Is All"; Cluff's "I Am Praying for You"; Havergal's "Light After Darkness"; and Cushing's "O, Safe to the Rock!"

Sankey's music to Miss Elizabeth C. Clephane's "The Ninety and Nine" was composed under the most dramatic of circumstances. This young Scotland woman's life, marked by deep suffering, was followed by her death at the age of thirty-nine, in 1869—five years before Sankey sang her into immortality. On May 20, 1874, Sankey and Moody were in the Glasgow railway station, waiting for a train to Edinburg, where they were to hold a three-days series of meetings, beginning May 21. Sankey bought a penny newspaper. Among the *advertisements* he found Miss Clephane's poem "The Ninety-and Nine," composed in 1868. He clipped it, pasted it into the Seed Plot, and read it to Moody, who was unimpressed. Two days later, at noon, Moody was speaking in the Free Assembly Hall upon "The Good Shepherd." Bonar followed Moody. When Bonar finished, Moody said, "Sankey, have you an appropriate solo?"

[2]This tune must not be confused with the more familiar one by Maker.

Guidance came powerfully upon Sankey to "sing the clipping." Yet, to do that meant stark improvising; there was no music. "He lifted his heart in prayer, opened the Seed Plot to the clipping, and began in A Flat."

> There were ninety and nine that safely lay
> In the shelter of the fold,
> But one was out on the hills away,
> Far off from the gates of gold.

The first verse went well. He wondered if he could repeat the melody on the second. He did, note for note. And it has not been changed to this day! The great sigh that went up from the vast audience, and the sobs of thousands, bore testimony that Zion had a new song.

In later years, Sankey produced a stack of melodies. *Gospel Hymns Nos. I to VI*, print the astonishing number of nearly eighty-most of which miss immortality by a wide margin. But in this later group are the well-known tunes for Bonar's "A Shelter in the Time of Storm," Cooper's "While the Days Are Going By," and Annie Herbert's "When the Mists Have Rolled Away."

Some of the other songs highly valuable to Sankey were Whittle and McGranahan's five-star productions, "I Know Whom I Have Believed," "There Shall Be Showers of Blessing," "I Shall Be Satisfied." In this connection we note another by Major Daniel Webster Whittle (El Nathan) written in Chicago during the Columbian Exposition, 1893, his daughter May Whittle (Mrs. W. R. Moody) supplying the melody, the unusually sweet song, "Moment By Moment."

By 1880 Sankey had added to his collection, Geo. C. Stebbin's music for Edmeston's "Saviour Breathe an Evening Blessing," Alexander's "There Is a Green Hill Far Away," Morgan's "Fully Trusting," and the anonymous "I've Found a Friend."

Gospel Hymns Consolidated, grouping *Gospel Hymns and Sacred Songs* (Sankey's first book, 1873), and *Gospel Hymns No. 2* by Sankey and Bliss, and *Gospel Hymns Nos. 3 and 4* by Sankey, McGranahan and Stebbins, print the following "sure fires"; Atkinson and Main's "We Shall Meet Beyond the River," Cushing and Root's "Ring the Bells of Heaven" and "When He Cometh," Lowry's distinctive music for Watts' "We're Marching to Zion," "Where Is My Boy Tonight?" and "Shall We Gather at the River?" For the last two named, Lowry composed both words and music.

But "The Mighty Man" in Sankey's repertoire was Paul Phillip Bliss. The centennial of his birth will arrive July 9, 1938. A considerable amount of attention has recently been given-and properly-to the music of Stephen Collins Foster. It is unthinkable that Bliss should fail to have equal attention in 1938. Where Foster's music is sung by thousands, Bliss' is sung by tens of thousands. He was in every way "a bright and shining light." Moody's decision to have a singer of his own came to him while listening to Bliss' rich voice in Farwell Hall in 1869. The royalties on *Gospel Hymns and Sacred Songs,* which Bliss and Sankey issued in 1875, ran to $60,000; and they gave it away! Moody said, "Bliss, you ought to keep $5,000." Bliss replied, "Not one cent! it all belongs to God!" On December 29, 1876, this talented young musician and his equally talented wife, Lucy J. Young, both under forty, were killed in a railway wreck at Ashtabula, Ohio.

But he left a heritage of church music which is immortal; and which was the very foundation of Sankey's great career. Just think of these songs coming from one man, *words and music*. "Almost Persuaded"; "Dare to Be a Daniel"; "Free from the Law"; "Hallelujah, He Is Risen"; "Hold the Fort"; "Hallelujah, What a Saviour"; "Jesus Loves Even Me"; "Let the Lower Lights Be Burning"; "More Holiness Give Me"; "Only an Armor Bearer"; "Pull for the Shore"; "Roll On, O Billow of Fire"; "Whosoever Will" and "The Light of the World Is Jesus."

In addition to this *partial* list, McGranahan wrote the music for Bliss' "That Will Be Heaven for Me," and Bliss wrote the music for Hearn's "Waiting and Watching," Oakley's "What Shall the Harvest Be," and the anonymous "Go Bury Thy Sorrow." His fame is as secure as that of the composer of "My Old Kentucky Home."

* * *

After a few weeks of the English Revival, Sankey's music became so popular that he was beset with the difficulties arising from loaning his scrap-book and not getting it back in time for meeting.

Partially to solve the difficulty, he tried to get the publishers of Philip Phillips' *Hallowed Hymns* to make a supplement of Sankey's collection. This they refused to do. "Mr. Phillips was away on his concert tour in California." D. L. took the matter in hand. Sankey cut twenty-five pieces from his scrap-book, rolled them up, and wrote thereon, *Sacred Songs and Solos Sung by Ira D. Sankey at the Meetings of Mr. Moody of Chicago.*

Moody went off to London to get a printer. For several hours he heard various Britishers say, "Sorry old chap; but I cawn't, you know." Finally "a printer in a cellar" stated, "I'll do it, but I must have the money in advance." It took every cent Moody and Sankey had. But the first edition sold out in a few hours; and from then on the presses rolled day and night, "building the schools in Northfield, and the edifices of the Chicago institutions."

G. T. B. Davis, a careful authority, states that in 1900 the royalties on one of the later song-books, *Gospel Hymns and Sacred Songs,* reached a million and a quarter dollars, "one of the best paying literary properties in the world." Moody and Sankey retained the royalties for personal use until January 1, 1875; the amounts received up to that time were more than sufficient for all their needs. One is convinced that this sum was adequate, when he learns that the royalties to September, 1885, were $357,-338.64. After January 1, 1875, the money was "received by a committee and applied to religious purposes in the United States." The committee of trustees for distributing this money was W. E. Dodge, George Stuart, and J. V. Farwell.

What a publisher's romance these song-books made! The circulation in the various editions ran into millions of copies, and the royalties were "incredibly large." Compare this with the most recent figures upon the business of book printing in America.[3] Here, for instance, is that small group of writers known as

> "the best sellers, whose books, usually fiction, mount to 50,000-once in a blue moon to 100,000-copies. In 1934, there were exactly fifteen authors whose books sold 500,000 copies or more in America. Only sixty-five titles have sold 500,000 or more in America since 1875."

But, we understand how thoroughly the church began to sing, when we remember that the Moody and Sankey hymnals went into the millions. Sankey used his part of the royalties, which were his own property by every right, in a magnificent way, to help Moody's great institutions; and in addition, he had some projects of his own, as for instance a $40,000 Y. M. C. A. building, and a lot for his beloved church, in the old home-town.

* * *

For a quarter of a century this pair of lowly, Spirit-filled men moved upon the hearts of the millions of people in their audiences. Then came to

[3]Quotations from Edward Week's engaging book, *This Trade of Writing*, Little, Brown and Company. 1935.

Sankey the heavy sorrow of that day in December, 1899, when his chief, whom he loved with such singleness of heart, lay fallen in Israel. From then on he was a broken man. In 1903, as a result (according to his own estimate) of services of "Sacred Song and Story" in thirty cities and towns in Great Britain, "my health broken down . . . and," he adds with infinite pathos, "*I lost my eyesight.*"

Five heavy years dragged on for the blind singer in his Brooklyn home. A ray of light came to his shadowed life one Sunday afternoon in the spring of 1907 when Dr. F. B. Meyer paid him a visit. Meyer held Sankey's hand and wept silently as he gazed into the wistful face and blind eyes. They talked over the golden days agone, when D. L. was with them. . . As Meyer rose to go he led Sankey over to the little melodeon and whispered, "Sing again, Beloved."

The shrunken fingers touched the yellowed keys; the old voice warmed slowly into something like its ancient beauty. And Meyer sobbed like a child when the faithful words filled the room:

> There'll be *no dark valley*
> When Jesus comes!

*   *   *

On a heated day of middle August, 1908, a little group tearfully waited in the home of the dying man. Once again he was in Scotland, practising, the window open, with the throngs outside. . . He was just doing his best to sing for his chief, but, somehow he couldn't find the place. . . He *must* find a song. . . Ah, here it is:

"Only an Armor-bearer!"

Well, that was fitting. He *was* just that to D. L. and glad to be. . . Circling angels bore him home to glory. Now he had his eyes again . . . but it was so strange . . . the thousands gone before who had been won in the meetings were acclaiming *him*, just as if *he* had led them to Christ. . . They ought to know better; it was D. L. . . And in the midst of his sweet confusion he stood before a throne and beheld One he had been anxious all these years to see, *Face to Face!* And he heard the Lamb of God speaking to *him:*

> "Well done, good and faithful servant! You esteemed yourself only an armor-bearer! But all service ranks the same with me. Receive that glory immortal and the bright crown of which thy lips so often sang!"

XV
THE WORLD TURNS ASIDE
(1873-1879)

Undoubtedly York was settled on its lees when Moody and Sankey arrived. This town of *fifty* thousand had sittings for *seventy-five thousand* in its more than forty churches and chapels! But, the inhabitants, by the large, were so well educated religiously, so decent,–and so dead! And now,–come Moody and Sankey to change it!! "What could the citizens of York want of uncultivated revivalists, who had never been ordained or even licensed to preach!"–*Sketch Book.*

————————————

"When God wants to move a mountain, He does not take a bar of iron, but He takes a little worm. The fact is, we have got too much strength. We are not weak enough. It is not our strength that we want. One drop of God's strength is worth more than all the world. Some one said, 'I cannot be anything more than a farthing rushlight.' Well, be that! that is enough!"–*D. L. M. opening sermon, Hippodrome Meetings, New York, 1876.*

THE WORLD TURNS ASIDE
(1873-1879)

The good news D. L. brought back to Chicago in September, 1872-the invitations to hold English meetings-came just in time. Sankey was on the point of going to California on a concert tour with Philip Phillips, but he and his wife reconsidered and decided to go to England with the Moodys. Everything was all settled, save the arrival of the necessary traveling expenses from the English friends. Someone said to Moody, "You've just been to England. Why go back so soon?" And he replied, "To win ten thousand souls for Christ!"

But the promised fare did not come. Month after month of stony silence, until September, 1872, shifted to May, 1873. Moody then felt God wanted him and Sankey to get to England any way they could. So he retrieved four hundred and fifty dollars he had invested. Not quite half enough, but they would "get going and see how it turned out." On June 4, 1873, they boarded the train for New York, still lacking steamship passage. But before the train pulled out of the station, John Farwell put his personal check for five hundred dollars into Moody's hand, "You may need it when you get to England." Moody grinned to himself. "Yes, indeed! I'll need to *get* to England." Nine hundred and fifty dollars was just enough.

On June 7, 1873, the dapper little *City of Paris* put out from New York for Liverpool. There is a deck picture in the Washburne Collection worth a hearty smile–two plump ministerial young gentlemen, in a going-away pose, their ruddy, almost English faces covered to the cheek bones with dark beards and moustaches. One feels like urging young Mr. Moody (now thirty-six) to enjoy himself while he is able. He was a notoriously poor sailor; "got sick when he bought his ticket." Almost immediately after clearing the harbor, he disappeared to his cabin for the rest of the trip. Sankey said, "He did so for good and sufficient reasons."

The ship landed at Liverpool June 17. "Immediately they found out why the English brethren never sent the expense money. A letter placed in Moody's hand stated that Pennyfather and Bainbridge were both dead. Later, they found Bewley, too, had died. Sankey was completely dismayed. "It was anything but cheerful. Here we were in a strange country, without an invitation, no committee and mighty little cash."

Moody held the bad-news letter in his hand and said, "If the Lord opens a door, we'll go through. If not, we'll go back to America." He then tried to park the letter in a bulky mass already in his coat pocket. It didn't fit well, so he took the entire jumble out for rearrangement. Right on top lay a letter he "had neglected to open in New York." He read it and said immediately, "We'll stay. Here's a partly open door."

"Partly open," was divinely accurate. The letter came from George Bennett, "Honorary Secretary" of the Y. M. C. A. at York. By way of making a living, Mr. Bennett had a small apothecary's shop, with quarters above—and "no lift."

The letter was a vague proposal that if Mr. Moody should come that way sometime, he might preach a few days. Moody wired Bennett, "I'm ready to begin." Bennett replied. "Religion at low ebb here. Will take a month to get ready." Moody answered, "I'll be in York tonight!"

The Moodys and Sankeys separated to meet in York, the Sankeys going to the home of Henry Moorhouse; the Moodys to the home of Emma's London sister. When Sankey arrived in York three days later, he found Mr. Bennett at work in his little shop, "completely bowled over . . . he didn't expect them so soon . . . everybody was away at the beach . . . no time at all to try meetings." Sankey said, "Where's Moody?" And with a gesture of despair, Bennett pointed his thumb at the ceiling just above him. Moody had already arrived.

Sankey wrote in his autobiography that Moody didn't show the slightest sign of anxiety. "After talking over the situation awhile, he asked Mr. Bennett to secure permission to use an Independent Chapel." Moody hustled off to see the pastor; arrangements were made, and on Thursday evening, June 22, 1873, the services began. "Less than fifty present! they took their seats as far away from the pulpit as possible! They wouldn't sing; they didn't take to the little organ, or the Yankee tunes."

And thus began the greatest revival since Pentecost!

The next day Moody launched noon prayer-services and Bible meetings in "a small upper room (over the drug-store) reached through a gloomy hall." Six people present. Seven days later an English dominie, with the finely cut features of a young Isaiah, arose and testified: "What Mr. Moody says about the Holy Spirit for service is true. I have been preaching for years, toiling hard, beating the air; no power. For two past days I've been away closeted with my Master. I've prayed, 'Oh God, give me the Holy Spirit.' . . Well, my Lord has had the victory over me, and I have made a full surrender." And that youngster later became known as the author of *Israel, a Prince with God*—F. B. Meyer.

Young Meyer opened his Baptist Chapel for Moody's services and instantly, to Sankey's profound amazement, the great revival began. "The Lord smote the rock in the desert of doubt and unbelief at York and hundreds filled the inquiry room." From these small beginnings the splendor of God abode until the attendance reached twenty thousand in Agricultural Hall two years later.

It requires inflexible determination to discard my thoroughgoing notes upon the great meetings in England and America during the next six years. What a vast chronicle it is! Really, it is an almost intolerable burden to spend the weary hours reading, reading, reading those hundreds of pages; the exalted monotony of it all; Moody preaching the same sermons, in almost the same order, to congregations alike in vastness and spiritual reactions; the ten thousand events in the lives of individuals which show the redemptive power of the gospel. It makes an evangelical Froissart's Chronicle which most men warmly praise–to escape reading.

Well, we discard these Bollandic records, not in deprecation of Moody's labors, but in a humble copying of The Writer, who, mindful of our frailty, cut down the super-world library detail of the King's labor into Four Readable Narratives. The deepest purpose of this book is to observe the hand of God transforming the worm Jacob into a new, sharp threshing-instrument, having teeth. One feels sure that the Holy One desires our attention chiefly upon *the hour of transition,* not upon volumes which would be necessary to record, after the transition, how he threshed the mountains, beating them small, esteeming the hills but chaff. Every line therefore, unnecessary to this purpose, is to be rubbed out.

*   *   *

The great revival in England continued for slightly more than two years, from the landing of the Moody party, June 17, 1873, to their return to New York on the S. S. *Spain,* August 4, 1875. It was a triumphal march.

York, Sunderland, Newcastle-on-Tyne, Edinburg, where they began on a dismal night with an overflow house, and so continued until "almost every Christian household had been blessed with one or more conversions." (Horatius Bonar.)

Glasgow, where three thousand joined the

churches and seventeen thousand signed the pledge; Perth, Aberdeen, Tain, Huntley, where he spoke to fifteen thousand in the open air.

Rothesay; Belfast, "where he spoke to six acres of Irishmen"; Londonderry; Dublin, where Catholic priests attending in a body said, "Sure, and if it's a little longer they're staying, St. Patrick will be supplanted by a Yankee."

Manchester; Sheffield; Birmingham; Liverpool, where they built the first temporary tabernacle-eleven thousand capacity!

London with four revival centers, and a total attendance of 2,330,000!

The crowds in all these meetings were overwhelming. Jessie McKinnon describes them:

> "One gets accustomed to crowds. What at one time excited feelings of surprise is now taken as a matter of course. But the spectacle itself is just the same,-full of moral grandeur, and at most times felt with an intensity and earnestness too much for one to carry, and to be cast on God whose work it is."

Some one else described how the crowds got to the meetings, in a day before autos:

> "Vehicles were not easily to be had on Sunday, so nearly all came on foot,-gentle and simple, young and old, blind and lame. Many a time the Great Western Road had been blackened for an hour and a half with this living stream;

one night when twenty thousand were present, this stream flowed three hours."

The expenses of the party for the entire English visit were met by royalties upon the hymn-books sold in Scotland and Ireland up to January 1, 1875. We are glad to take the mystery out of this question. Some idea as to the adequacy of this fund will be gained by noting that in the six months after January 1 the royalties, which were no longer kept for personal use, amounted to $27,092.

*   *   *

The Moodys landed in New York August 14,1875, and rushed to Northfield, August 16. He and Emma had come to some important conclusions en route. It was plain that his Chicago days were over; his was now a world mission. Northfield, "the most beautiful village in the world," would be an ideal home center. He would always be as a father to the beloved Chicago Church, but now it must be placed entirely in other hands.

Arriving in Northfield, the now world-famous evangelist was phlegmatically received. Ed met him at the depot, then drove the family up to the birthplace in an old rickety buggy. During the lovely Northfield summer of 1875, he began his annual summer practice of reading the Bible through, "to tune the instrument." One day "he abruptly purchased twelve acres and a house just beside the Birthplace," at thirty-five hundred dollars, largely because "his mother's chickens were annoying the neighbor." His original idea was to keep "a chicken run" and sell the rest. But he found "he liked it mighty well." So he kept it. . . And the world today, passing by the lofty screening lilac hedges, says, "That's Moody's home!" Of which a bit more, in the intimate Chapter XXII, "He Groweth Much Heavenward."

*   *   *

On October 24, 1875, he began an American Apostolate, extending over a period of about four years, quite up to the high level of the English campaign. And once again we exclude from the pages of this volume the extensive notes in the *Sketch Book,* as not being necessary to the aim in mind. But, it will repay any one who takes the time to read the details for himself. We trace, therefore, the larger outline only.

The itinerary included Brooklyn (which dates the beginning of the Great Awakening of 1876); Philadelphia (held in a vast, old freight depot, belonging to John Wanamaker and set in order for the meetings by him; such a rain-deluge the opening night, that over the banks went the Schuylkill-and nine thousand present!); New York (total attendance a million and a half; three thousand joined the churches); Augusta; Chicago (where the old home town waived the rule of no honor to the native prophet); Boston (these meetings caused young A. J. Gordon to find himself, just as it happened to his friend, F. B. Meyer in York); St. Louis (where things happened to C. I. Scofield!).

The meetings in the foregoing larger cities were followed by similar triumphs in smaller places during 1877-1878: Burlington, Montpelier, Concord, Manchester, Providence, Springfield (Mass.), Hartford, New Haven. In October, 1878, he began in Baltimore, and preached for months in various churches, (here, during meetings on April 11, 1879, Paul Dwight Moody was born).

These "Mighty Six Years" in England and America bring us up to the summer of 1879, when D. L. began an entirely new phase of his career, symbolized by the employment of his father's trowel in laying the corner-stone of the first building, Northfield Seminary. The dramatic sequence is again set aside at the close of this chapter, in order to analyze certain dramatic phases of Moody's evangelical technique; and it is resumed in Chapter XX, "Pilgrim Takes Up a Trowel."

*   *   *

This broad-brush sketch of "The Mighty Six" leaves out of composition the amazing personnel of men and women who worked with him—scholars, nobility, statesmen, labor leaders, ministers, merchants, artists, people who rallied about Moody "to hold up his hands." Imperfect amends are made in Chapter XXIII, titled "And Is Compassed About By a Cloud of Witnesses."

And the bitter contempt, studied opposition, each of which ended in futility, is left out of composition entirely. This was one romantic chapter I feared to submit to my overburdened Judson Pressmen—"Pilgrim Meets Apollyon, And Goes Off With the

Field!" Yea, verily, and there are half a dozen other orphaned chapters!

By 1876 the world awoke to the fact that a new volume was being added to The Romance of the Church. And it rubbed its eyes in bewilderment as it observed that the two dominating figures were certainly not of the mighty, or cultured, or highly talented. Yet seldom since Pentecost and certainly not since Wesley and Whitefield did such a phenomenon appear. Every movement Moody and Sankey made, every word uttered, was read to the ends of the earth. By the mystery of Godliness in them, they lifted the weight of stagnant and dead religion in America and England, negativing for a period of almost thirty years the effective spread of "the small black plague spot of German Paralysis called Destructive Criticism." Of course, to use the dainty words of Scotch Jimmie Barrie, "It got us in the end!" But these two fought it back until almost 1900.

How *did* they do it? How did *they* do it? Moody and Sankey, growing humbler with every increment of world power, knew the answers to both questions. In the beginning of the meetings in the New York Hippodrome, February 7, 1876, Moody answered; answered in terms of the Burning Bush:

> "God hath chosen the weak things of the world to confound the mighty,–that no flesh should glory in His presence. Let us take our place in the dust, and give God the glory! When God delivered Egypt, He didn't send an army. *We would*

have sent an army, or an orator! But God sent *a man*, who had been in the deserts forty years, and had an impediment in his speech. It is *weakness* that God wants! *Nothing* is small when God handles it. God wants us to ask great things of Him. Pray, 'Oh, God, give *me* the Holy Spirit!'"

XVI
He Continually Looks at His Scroll

There is real consolation in Moody's life for those of us who at the beginning did neither choose the right way nor walk therein. Like Bunyan's Pilgrim,-and ourselves!-he thought so much of what he heard from men, that his Scroll fell from his bosom, and for some time he missed it not. And lo! it was a healing ministry to him,-as it is to us!-to come thereby to a great distress; thus to fall on his knees, to ask God's forgiveness for his foolish fact, and to go back, and to look for it.

Yea, it was a great day for him when like Israel he was made to tread those steps thrice over which he needed not to have trod but once. And it was a greater day when, weeping, he espied his Scroll, which he with trembling and haste snatched up . . . put in his bosom! . . gave thanks to God . . . with joy and tears betook himself again to his journey. But oh, how nimbly now did he go up the rest of the hill! And whensoever thereafter, he had need of refreshment, or of inspiration, or of Wisdom, he did continually look at his Scroll.-*Sketch Book.*

He Continually Looks at His Scroll

We commonly dismiss that morning freshness of natural leaders with a word, *originality*. But, actually, what is it? Whence comes it? What made it? If we can recover the rapt astonishment of a little child, which receives kingdoms, we suddenly discover that *originality* is simply *getting back* to origins; not the *creation thereof*. Whosoever, therefore, sets his heart to possess this pearl of great price, will school himself to pass by what a thousand and one have said about a subject, and will fill himself full of the thing where it *started*.

And at no point does this discipline bear such golden sheaves as when applied to the Bible. But, alas, at no point have we been such chronic hamartites! Aye! what infatuation is this that leads us, who wish to be Christ's under-teachers, to treat the Bible as if it were a spiritual Roget, to be used as a now-and-then reference, not as a book for reading? Merci! it has well-nigh done for us, yielding a contemporary leadership, cold as a glacial night. Where have we been looking to miss the dramatic way in which a man fires up, when he snuffs out his two-penny tapers from the Candle of the Month Club, and turns to the Light of the Word! Here we have the explanation of the annoying vitality of Bible Institutes (cross yourselves, gentlemen, as at the name of the devil!), while "Standard Schools" remain safe, obedient, polite and sterile.

Sure, and Some One has set forth Moody as a witness
unto this contention. There was a wide time when he used
texts as cotton cords upon which to string his pretty glass
beads, even as you and I. But when he came to himself, he
saw his Father's hired servants had full hampers, while he
and his dependents went hungry. So he arose and
returned, not without hard going; returned, to that
established policy of making the Bagster his vade mecum.
He stocked his soul with the purple and fine linen
thereof. He came to admire the Writings so deeply, that
he invited every statement he made to seek a garment
from Solomon's Wardrobe. Suddenly this common man
had about him a strange light. *The world* marveled: "He's
original!" Little did it dream where he was getting his
cedar beams, his rafters of fir, and his odor of myrrh. You
see, the world doesn't read Canticles. And the few right-
dividers who heard him, and *knew*, admired him yet the
more for his wisdom!

*   *   *

Henry (Harry) Moorhouse must be credited, under
God, for thrusting Moody toward Bible greatness. This
puny Lancashire lad lived less than forty years; burned
himself to a cinder. Born in Ardwich, in 1840, he was hell-
bent-on-high by the time he was twenty; a cocky little
bantam-weight prizefighter, battling equally vs. men and
alcohol. At nineteen he was done for. One night, in an
excess of remorse, he stood in a dark hall toying with a
loaded pistol. Some one was holding a little meeting over-

head, door open; he heard a voice reading the Prodigal Son, and the mystery of conviction covered his poor soul. Just the Word! And a few weeks later, a faithful fireman in a Manchester warehouse basement brought him to light with Romans 10:9, 10. Just the Word!

He at once began to witness with *just the Word* in the mission rooms. No one "cared enough about the little runt" to suggest a course of study. So he kept to just the Word; soaked it up; flavored himself therewith to the fingertips. Within four years, he was a bright and shining light. Men from every strata, burly colliers or brainy courtiers, sat spellbound before him. In 1879 his health crumbled. Physicians told him, "You must stop–your heart!" "How long will I live if I stop?" "Probably eighteen months." "And if I keep on?" "Perhaps nine months." "Very well, I'll take the nine months, and preach Christ as long as I can." On December 25, 1880, he spent his first Christmas in heaven, after twenty years of incredibly fruitful ministry in the Word, intercessory prayer, and life changing.

When he met Moody in England in 1867, he "loved him at once, but saw he was deficient in the Word." He proposed returning with Moody to America, but D. L. "gave him the slip," and sailed without him. Nevertheless, he trailed him back to Chicago on practically the next boat. He frankly told D. L., "You're on the wrong tack"; then *proved* it by some spectacular meetings in Moody's church. Moody had that same savage annoyance that the rest of us feel when we collide with men of that type; but Moody had the grace to snap out of it.

Snapping out of it, however, did not achieve a faultless obedience to his heavenly vision. It was a blood-struggle for him to acquire in perpetuity the mental frame enjoined in, "To the Law and to the Testimony." It meant patient, ceaseless, determined struggle. Some one said, "How can I learn to use the Bible that way?" He said, "*Arouse* yourself to it! Plead with God; He'll assuredly help you."

He found immediately that to effect a cure, he must begin first and foremost with a resolution to master just what the Bible *says*. He must abandon his hot haste to read a text, and then tell what it *taught*. This showed him at once that he had a Dives poverty in knowing what the Bible actually *said*. Then he awoke to the startling truth that no man can possibly tell what the Bible *teaches* until he has a lawyer's accuracy in quoting exactly what it *says*—reels of it; pages of it! And his heart smote him to think of the farcical character of his preaching, when he had a vast amount to say *about* a text, which to save his life he couldn't accurately *quote*. (Ever note the calamity which descends when a modern Apollos traps himself into trying to quote a text in the middle of his sermon?)

This excellent insistence upon "what does it *say*, never mind what you think it teaches," brought certain remarkable attitudes. He would repeatedly say, "Tell us your experience in *Bible* language." If some one attempted to state a religious *teaching*, he would promptly ask, "Have you God's *Word* for it?"

He saw, furthermore, that the handling of the Word to which he aspired meant the rigid, stern employment of *one* personal copy.

> "I have carried *one* Bible with me a great many years. It is worth a great deal to me, and I will tell you why: because I have so many passages marked in it."

This old Bible wore out entirely. An interleaved was purchased somewhere in the eighties, the old markings copied, additional ones added, and from the interleaved, in 1895, the Fleming H. Revells issued the widely circulated *Notes from My Bible.* Mel Trotter owns that Bible now, presented to him by Paul Dwight Moody. Trotter writes me, March 28, 1936,

> "It is very dear to me! But it is getting so worn I am not carrying it any more. I expect to give it to Moody Bible Institute. . . I think that is the place for it."

What a fine fog we of this day have gotten ourselves into by acting the part of homiletical humming-birds, darting from one translation to another, ignorant of all of them! Well, until we know the Book in *one* version, we'd do well to dispense with the rest. Out the windows with all of them, from the George Ade Vernaculars to the Short Fuzzy Kants (Mayhem editions). And the commentaries with them, until we're *ready* to use them; and have learned *how.*

Moody's innocence of these numerous versions, that now fly up at us from our shelves like mosquitoes, left him no choice but the King James. So he girded his loins to master just what the King James *said*. This meant arising at four a.m. for two hours of Bible reading. "I have reason for believing," said Torrey, "that Moody rose thus early to the close of his life. He would say, 'If I am going to get in any Bible study, I have got to get up before the rest of the folks get up.'" And when he *studied* the Bible, he studied the *Bible*. "I pour over the pages, not through the specs of some learned commentator, but with my own eyes."

He felt also that the large bulk of his Bible reading should be in that consecutive decent form accorded to any other type of literature. "What would you know of your boy's letter if you were to read the superscription on Monday, signature Friday, and a little in the middle three months later?"

Then, he was equally convinced that one should make much of topical study. "If I were going into a court of justice, I should get every witness to testify to the one point on which I wanted to convince the jury. So it should be with the scriptures." "I took up that word 'Love,' and I do not know how many weeks I spent in studying the passages in which it occurs, till at last I could not help loving people. It just flowed out my fingertips." "I got to thinking of the compassion of Christ. So I took the Bible and began to read it over to find out what it said on that subject. At last the thought of His infinite compassion overpowered me, and I could only lie on the floor of my study, with my face in the open Bible and cry like a child!"

To the foregoing methods he added an annual, intensive reading. "I get tired toward the end of July, and I go away to the mountains. I take the Bible with me. (Try it next summer on *your* vacation.) I read it through and I feel as if I had never seen the book before, it seems so new, so rich, so varied, the truth flashing from a thousand unexpected and undiscovered points with a light above the sun. That summer reading is what I call tuning the instrument."

*   *   *

The results of such reference to origins were transforming. Gradually he gave up any and all dependence upon human exhortations and anecdotes as a *means* of awakening sinners. He continued to use his effective stories, but, always to make a Bible passage clearer. He gave "Bible readings" as high prominence as he gave preaching services. He came "to believe in the Bible from back to back." It was the source of faith: "I used to think I should close my Bible and pray for faith: but I came to see it was in studying the Word of God, 'Faith cometh by hearing, and, hearing by the Word of God.'" Did a man wish to attract crowds? Well, get back to the Bible! "Don't you think *God* knows how to interest people?" It was the final court of authority: "Do you know what I do when any man preaches against the doctrines I preach? . . I go to the Bible . . . if I am right, I give them more of the same kind."

The mighty torrent of his love for the Book is to be seen in his first present to his first grandchild, Baby Irene, born August 20, 1895, died August 22, 1899. A part of the tender little inscription runs, "The Bible for the last forty years has been the dearest thing on earth to me, . ."

*   *   *

Small wonder that his preaching had that fresh April wonder of first century thinking. Small wonder that men of highest mental endowment followed him respectfully; he possessed that refinement which comes only from the Mighty Hammer and the Excellent Fire.

*   *   *

In the nineties, he became aware that the church was losing her radiance. He knew where the trouble lay–her leaders were repudiating the Bible. And men like Lyman Abbott, himself a repudiator, foresaw also just what was going to happen:

> "Evolution has revolutionized our conception of the origin of sin and the nature of the Bible. I do not believe in the infallibility of the book with Mr. Moody. . . But if we of liberal faith hope to retain the attractive power of the church, we can do it only by holding fast the great spiritual facts(!) . . . if we fail, men will desert our ministry for Romanism or Anglicanism . . . or in despair men will desert us altogether, and live a

wholly material life alternating between unsatisfied desire and sated self-content." (Abbott, editorial in *Outlook*, 1900.)

We behold the followers of Lyman Abbott, today, almost alone in their Pewish Wailing Places, having failed either "to hold fast the great spiritual facts," or "to dramatize what they had left!"

But Moody so much disliked "to draw circles that left men out," that he held to some of these leaders against his own misgivings. Of such was Henry Drummond. The inclusion of Drummond, and others of his kind, like George Adam Smith, on Moody's programs, was a stumbling-block to many. When the storm of criticism began to arise, Moody tried to justify Drummond in the statement, "I have never heard or read anything by Drummond with which I did not heartily agree–*though I wish he would speak more often of the atonement.*" Drummond declined longer to appear on Moody's programs when the 1893 Chicago campaign was arranged. "It was the first time Drummond failed me." But Drummond's good judgment kept him from exposing Moody to further attacks. For it was only Moody's lack of information–"never read anything"–that kept Drummond in his favor.

Drummond was one of the vanguard of men, amiable, attractive, to whom no one could deny the name Christian, who nevertheless helped write "Ichabod" over Twentieth Century Zion. Dr. C. W. Petty[1] accurately describes his kind as "Religious

[1]*Today's Jesus*, Judson Press.

leaders proud to be altar boys to the priests of science . . . exhibiting a pathetic, if not humiliating manner of pouncing on every friendly statement science makes about faith."

The servility into which Drummond fell can best be observed in his own words.[2]

"Theology now proceeds by asking Science what *it* demands, and then borrows its instruments. I name two-the Scientific Method and the Doctrine of Evolution . . . *that this doctrine is proved yet no one will assent* . . . yet, we cannot be too grateful to Science for *this splendid hypothesis* (!) which fills a gap in the beginnings of our religion . . . by science evolution is the method of creation . . . likewise science expects revelation (the Bible) to be an evolution . . . it is important to assure science this same difficulty has been felt with equal keenness by theology . . . so we . . . of the scientific method . . . no more pledge ourselves to the interpretation of the Bible of a thousand years ago than does Science the interpretation of Pythagoras. Evolution has given us a clearer Bible. . . The difficulties (of reconciling many things in the Bible with our ideas of a holy God) arise from old-fashioned, or unscientific views . . . when by new view-points these difficulties are seen to be rudiments of truth spoken in strange ways to attract and teach *children* (!) . . .

[2]George Adam Smith, *The Life of Henry Drummond*.

"Christianity knows it can approve itself to Science, but has been taken by surprise and therefore begs time. It will honestly look up its credentials and adjust itself!" (all italics mine).

There would be no justification in calling to mind this compromising page from Yesterday, unless it were used as an Egyptian stone. No man ever loved Moody more than did the gentle, devout, high-minded little Scotch professor. So long as time shall last, his *The Greatest Thing in the World* will be a high peak on the sky-line of devotional literature. But his Stultified Zone wherein Faith fawns over stuffed hypotheses from a Darwinian Museum and Credulity prefers the gourd-rattling of Lamarkian Medicine Men to the Voice of God—let us resolve to keep silence until the distemper has passed! Remember, it was the Chief Bad Man who advised, "I'll have some Binomic Pulp ask the Dominie to write a Religious Article—then I've got him!"

George Adam Smith rewarded Moody's open-handed hospitality with a sophomore's compliment: "Much of Moody's teaching repels a whole side of the church . . . diminishes his authority with thinking men and women . . . yet his *great personality*," etc., etc.

These pages out of yesterday ought to help us reaffirm without compromise a Supernatural Revelation. We are to be men well aware that science and faith are in different realms. We need not fear science, nor attack it, nor court its favor. And we are not to care a tinker's hemstitch over "diminishing our authority with *thinking* men and women." Moody's words on the Bible at this point are as timely as if uttered to a moribund church over this afternoon's national hook-up:

> "Thirty years ago people did not question the gospel. They believed that the Lord Jesus Christ, by dying on the cross, had done something for them . . . And my work was to bring them to a decision to do what they already knew they ought to do.
>
> But all is different now.
>
> The question-mark is raised everywhere. There is need for teachers who shall begin at the beginning and show the people what the gospel is.
>
> WHAT WE NEED TODAY IS MEN WHO BELIEVE IN THE BIBLE FROM THE CROWN OF THEIR HEADS TO THE SOLES OF THEIR FEET: WHO BELIEVE IN THE WHOLE OF IT, THE THINGS THEY UNDERSTAND, AND THE THINGS THEY DO NOT UNDERSTAND!"

XVII
AND DERIVES ABIDING CONVICTIONS

Now Pilgrim, constantly abiding in the Word, was given to see that the Gospel is withal a very simple matter, set up about two great Facts,—"For I delivered unto you first of all that which I also received, how that Christ died for our sins, according to the scriptures; and that He was buried, and that He rose again the third day according to the scriptures." To be sure, a worthy setting forth of these caused him to labor as if he were building a universe. But he was also spared from polishing peach seeds; bestowing breadless labor on such topics as "Flowers in Foot Steps," or, "The Secret of Popularity."

And he perceived salvation came to a man when he was right as to the Cross and as to the Resurrection,—"Believe in thine heart that God hath raised him from the dead, [and] thou shalt be saved." But he also saw that the very simplicity of saving faith constituted the mystery of Godliness, so clear that a child could grasp it, yet so deep as to go beyond man's best thinking.—*Sketch Book.*

AND DERIVES ABIDING CONVICTIONS

Moody's surrender to the Word, "attendance to reading and wholly giving himself thereto," resulted in a profiting that appeared to all. Lo, it is amazing to note with how little he began and how great he thereby became. He best took heed unto himself by taking heed to the Teaching; and he waxed rich in the great convictions which a man *practically* holds. These convictions went far deeper than his mere argumentative area; they were treasures which he laid to heart, giving him assurance as to his arrival in the favor of God, and setting forth how he got there. They were sanctions upon which he confidently built his life, making him insensible to hardship, and creatively determining everything else. If he spoke as it were the Oracles of God, it was simply because his whole being had taken root upon the Truth as it is in Jesus.

One cannot read far into the extensive records of his doctrinal views, without noting that his theology was organized about two great facts—Christ *died* for our salvation, and *rose* for our justification. Everything else was subordinate.

He had a host of convictions, "in which he continued"; but all of them save Substitution and Resurrection were satellite. And he never suffered servants to dress like the prince.

Among the lesser lights were his views upon John Barleycorn. Thousands were influenced by his dramatic temperance dialogs, his strictures upon a social order that suffered alcohol to be commercialized. But he never let the Dry Camel nose him out of Evangel's Tent. Francis E. Willard said, "There's not sufficient temperance spirit in your meetings." D. L. replied, "If men are thoroughly regenerated, there's no use of the multitudinous measures you're advocating!" "After all, the *only hope* is that the Son of God has come to destroy man's appetite for drink." (D. L. M.)

He put a high value upon Christian education, and became a great figure as an educator. But he had an abrupt way of scrapping programs, when they began to savor of the Brain Trust, and substituting revivals.

How warm was his espousal of personal holiness! A Christian was in poor business at a theater; cards and the like were loaferish games; tippling was devilish. But he refused to use works as a gage for salvation; nay, "by grace are ye saved through faith; . . . it is the gift of God." Could a man be a Christian and smoke? Oh, yes. But naturally, he'd be a *dirty* Christian.

He had a very practical committal to social action, all the way from vast relief programs to "a quiet little visit to the City Hall, whereupon the abuse was stopped." But he had scant patience with Mr. Talkative Social Gospel, who lingered long in conference, making blue-prints for a New World, spinning subtleties that differentiated between *individual relief* and *social adjustment*. He heard the Resolutioneers in his day beginning to charge that the "old theology viewed suffering with indifference; it so emphasized soul salvation as to obscure social responsibility." He smiled while they fumed; finished his sermon on "Saved By Grace"; then went out and *did* what the Committee Boys were *talking* about.

He found much comfort in the hope of Christ's coming. To him, the Lord's return was imminent, visible, bodily and personal. "Christ returneth" was the only way to Millennial glory. This spared him from the Dreadful Let-Downs of Boot-Strap Theologians, who majored on that catchy Americanism–Making the world a better place to live in! "I look upon the world as a wrecked vessel, its ruin coming nearer and nearer. God has given me a life boat and said to me, 'Moody, save all you can.'" But his eschatology didn't cut the nerve-center of personal work, nor prevent him from building great institutions; neither did it set him to making tune-tables, nor identifying contemporary Mussolinis as the anti-Christ.

*   *   *

Take time to read carefully Moody's doctrinal utterances. Analyze and classify each statement. Make a graph embodying the whole of it; and that graph can be presented in the form of a hemispheric map, with the Atonement as the northern axis, and the Resurrection as the southern. The whole of his thinking revolved about these two poles.

Moody's sermon on the resurrection[1] is one of

[1]Number 24, *Colportage Library*. The reading of the twenty-one distinctively Moody books of this series is well worth while. Order them all at once for your centennial reading.

the few places where he talks at length upon that subject. Everywhere else the influence of the doctrine is observed in scattered sentences. But we plainly see that it was a bearing for his theology. "I never in my life saw a happy Christian who had doubts about the resurrection. Jesus arose from the dead! . . they had breakfast with Him. . . What a meal that was! How could they have been deceived about its being His real, identical body? Show me any one who does not believe that Christ has risen, and that the bodies of believers are to rise also, and I will show you a man who has very little comfort in his religion."

The salvation power of Christ was not yet completed in a Christian; his *body* was still carnal. Therefore, look out! The old Adam, our mortal body, was an enemy to our redeemed spirit. Some day, at Christ's coming, the body, too, was to be redeemed; but until then, it was invaluable to know that a Christian had two natures; this knowledge kept him from doubting his salvation, and kept him fighting for practical holiness.

* * *

But, Moody lived chiefly in the northern hemisphere, "Christ died for us." In the early days of the British revival, he responded to some who wanted to know his views, that they were already in print: "the fifty-third chapter of Isaiah." When in January, 1875, the revival was at its peak, he closed a Bible reading in Birmingham, on "The Blood of Christ," with these words: "If you wish to know the secret of our success for the last two years, it is this: we have stood fair and square on the Bible doctrine of Substitution. Oh! that is what is needed by a dying world, Substitution! If you take that out of the Bible, you can take the Bible along with you. The scarlet thread is unbroken from Genesis to Revelation."

Later he cried, "When I give up preaching Substitution, I shall go to farming, for I know not what else to preach." A Boston paper, surprised at his "creedal atavism" thus editorialized: "There is no longer any doubt as to Moody's doctrine. He is an out-and-out believer in the ruined state of man, and in pardon, through faith, in the substitution of the blood of Christ for broken law. *Evangelical religion never presented a bolder front!*" The death and the resurrection together, enabled him "to worship Jesus as God."

To him every great truth had its origin and meaning in the Atonement. Men could never be sons of God save by the cross. "I want to say emphatically I have no sympathy with the doctrine of universal brotherhood and universal Fatherhood. A man must be born into the household of faith by the Spirit, through Christ, before he becomes my brother, or a son of God."

Salvation was always and only the gift of God through faith in Christ crucified. When a man by faith accepted Substitution, "though like the crucified thief he could not lift hand or foot to help himself, yet Jesus would throw him a passport to Paradise." His redemption would be instant; "vile as hell one minute, saved the next"; "saved like Zaccheus, between the branches and the ground." This blood salvation had a wonderful effect upon men's characters: "they rarely remain subjects of charity, but rise at once to comfort and respectability." It was utterly impossible to make a man better by any other means: he must be born again by faith in Christ. And the greatest sin was not adultery, murder, or the like. It was rejection of the Cross, to be answered by eternal judgment; a subject upon which he could not speak without tears.

The ministry of the Spirit was a theme so attractive to Moody that hardly any sermon or address fails to bring it in. But the ministry of the Spirit had its headquarters in the Atonement. "I believe that if the Spirit had not come to men, the story of the life and death of Jesus would have died out." The Holy Spirit was *the* power in the gospel. "We cannot convict men of sin by any amount of logic, eloquence or human power. Conviction is the work of the Spirit only. I verily believe that if the mighty Angel Gabriel, who stands in the presence of God, were to come down from heaven, every hair blazing with the glory of that upper world, he could not convert a single sinner. Only the Spirit can do that." And *He does it* by "convicting the world of sin because they believe not" on the Cross.

Furthermore, if a Christian desires a deeper work of the Spirit, he must proclaim Christ crucified, "not himself, his notions, his theories and all that." When the Holy Spirit infills a Christian, "he is full of hope and cheer; ready for any work, and will not shirk the hard places." While he believed with all his heart that the infilling of the Holy Spirit was "something additional to conversion," yet he repudiated the idea that one such experience was a finality. "A great many think because they have been filled once, they are going to be full for all time after; but, O, my friends, we are leaky vessels, and have to be *kept right under the fountain all the time* in order to keep full. Some one asked a minister (no doubt D. L. himself) if he had ever received a second blessing since he was converted. 'What do you mean?' was the reply. 'I have received ten thousand since the first.'" (1876 Hippodrome Meetings.) "Let's pray for another; we need a fresh baptism, a fresh power, a fresh supply of grace, every time we take up a new task, go from one place to another." (Prayer-For-Power Service, Boston, 1877.)

The Spirit "was worth more than all the world to a Christian: He lights up the words that lie cold and still on the pages of the Bible, and makes them live and speak and work in us." If Christians did not have the Spirit, their "efforts were graceless, powerless: men were turned against the gospel."

But Christians must always remember that the Spirit is unwilling to testify through them unless, like the Spirit, they were glorifying Christ and His cross.

Ah, *everything* for Moody centered in the Atonement. He was fully committed to continue in it, for in so doing he could save himself and them that heard him. No other way! As far as he was concerned, Substitution was the touchstone of evangelical fellowship:

> "I will fellowship with any man who believes himself a sinner and trusts in Christ; but God being my helper, I will never fellowship a man that denies the deity of my God and Saviour, Jesus Christ, or sneers at His atonement."

XVIII
He Repairs to the Arsenal for His Arrows

Now for a long time Pilgrim fell miserably short of being a mighty hunter before Jehovah by reason of a foolish fact,- he continually shot flimsy arrows from the Tower of the Flock. Well did he know that Zion's storehouse had the finest materials; yet he by habit fashioned scrannel reeds for shafts, goose quills for barbs, and peacock feathers for tail-guides. Of course, it was rarely that any of the Lord's wounded were found after he fired his double dozen; but instead of setting a match to his humdrum missles, he carefully gathered them up for a reshooting.

Even after he came to himself, he found it desperately hard to overcome old custom. For long time, try as he would, he wrought just as the fletchers and bowyers of his day, and fashioned instruments sadly mixed; mayhap a Fiery Point at the tip, but a peacock feather on the tail piece. But his humiliation ended in the year that he bundled all his shortcomings, laid them before the King, and began crying, "O Lord! give me Thy Holy Spirit!" On a sudden he found blessed release; found that he had no further taste for aught save goods of the Arsenal. Then did his rejoicing spirit confess two wonders; that, though his new arrows were simple, compared with the old, yet when he put one of them on the string, the Holy One sent it right home!-*Sketch Book.*

He Repairs to the Arsenal for His Arrows

The pearl of great price in centennial thinking upon Moody's sermons is to be found in noting how, for long time, his preaching was powerless, and why; how tedious he found it to correct his shortcomings; and how impossibles were done when at last his message qualified. His sermons, like himself, had no more attraction than the millions of other wild acacias on the Sinaitic slopes, until the Word, which is like fire, got into the midst of them. This chapter requires, therefore, that every homiletic phase of Moody's ministry fall into rigid subordination to the foregoing thesis.

Of course it is rewarding to observe the foot-hills as we press to the summit, and this shall be swiftly done.

One of these captivating scenes on the way is a study of his progress as a public speaker. He seems always to have had the forensic instinct. "When Dwight was a little boy, he was fond of going into the garret and trying to make a speech all alone" (his mother to Richard C. Morse). G. T. B. Davis affirms that the first sermon was forced upon him: "The pulpit supply in North Market Hall failed to appear." When he began preaching, he couldn't remember his points very well; he "wanted to speak to intelligent people . . . they didn't like to hear me

. . . so I began with children (!)." He started with "crude mannerisms and much circumlocution." But he steadily "developed myself in cottage prayer-meetings, where I had the best hours of my life."

Gradually his ability to speak with telegraphic brevity increased, and his crudities vanished. Quiet power supplanted "March bluster." A histrionic presentation, compelling and unobjectionable, developed, until he was at the head of the list of contemporary, public speakers. In the Washburne Collection, there is an envelope addressed by D. L. to his brother Edwin, postmarked San Francisco, March 28, 1899. Within, there is a full-page clipping of the San Francisco *Examiner* showing Moody in four dramatic poses, and making a frank admission that he had unrivalled power as a natural, master dramatist.

These dramatic aspects of Moody in his heyday are well worth a quick survey. There he stands, a heavy, blunt fellow; superficially, one thinks there is no grace in look or action, until he has listened twenty minutes. We hear his words rushing from his bearded face like a torrent; often two hundred and thirty per minute; so fast it took four New York reporters in relay to "get him." Short staccato sentences; imperfect pronunciation. Spurgeon said, "the only man I ever knew who said 'Mesopotamia' in one syllable." We are aware of many "aints" and "have gots," but he is going so fast on something worth saying that we haven't time to worry. We are aware, too, of phrases oft repeated: he was always "sick and tired" of something or other; some Christian virtue was "more than all the world"; and if it were a question of tolerating an impossible, his left hand went up-"No! a thou-times, No!" Like his mother the most positive affirmation was made through the good Yankee phrase, "Well I *guess* I *do*." Yet there was something precious about these pet expletives to the thousands who loved him.

Jessie McKinnon narrated the story of a group of Scotch Christians walking together along the ocean, talking of the days when D. L. was preaching in Scotland. "Wasn't Christ near us?" "Could anyone ever forget?" Henry Drummond abruptly lifted his left hand and shouted, "No! a thousand times, No!" And the party laughed-then wept.

It seems he hardly starts to preach until he says, "Sankey, sing something." Really though, the watch says he has spoken thirty to forty minutes. He profoundly believed in brevity; he laughingly pictured a dominie preaching so long everybody left him, and then defended his length by saying, "It was a shame to stop while anybody was listening!" On rare occasions he spoke for an hour: but people didn't realize it. In Liverpool, "by some means the gas could not be lit, the fading twilight deepening into darkness made a scene intensely solemn; his earnest words awed the great multitude."

We observe, in passing, he had that captivating grace of "the unwitting shining countenance"; within a few moments love shines through, and our defences go down! ("If I can't stir up their love *with mine,* I don't get hold of them; if I do I never fail!")

We quickly pardon the husky, high key of his voice and the way he strains it. Yet we are awed to observe that fifteen thousand can hear him perfectly *out of doors,* as in Huntley, England . . . six acres of Irishmen get every word in Belfast . . . a vast multitude hangs spellbound at Rothesey; (spellbound on the Esplanade, "while twilight deepens into darkness, and the stars and lamps are reflected in the quiet waters"). We observe that voice can be ravishingly tender; he knew without being told that *tones* make all the difference between wounding and healing. And it could sound like the trumpet of doom. But we forget even his voice, as we wonderingly begin to hear within it the voice of Another. Yet fascinating as all that is, we have not reached the chief concern of this chapter.

*   *   *

We are surprised to discover that he has less than one hundred "choice spears." Actually there were about four hundred big manila envelopes, but less than a hundred were dearly beloved. These he repeated so often he ceased to care about repetition. And we are amazed to see the crowds follow him from one point to the other, twice or three times a day, *to hear him repeat.* With Jessie McKinnon, when we listen repeatedly to the same sermon, we feel the *power* as keenly as ever "though of necessity the *newness* has passed." And when we try to track down this perennial vitality, we get the rewarding discovery that he travailed again in pain until each repeated sermon was reborn in prayer.

The records of yesterday put blue ribbons on the following of his arrows: "Where Art Thou?" "Lifting Up the Son of Man," and "The Compassion of Our Lord." George Pentecost's choices were, "God Is Love," and "Sowing and Reaping." These to him represented, at the best, the two aspects of Moody's messages to sinners. My own favorites—of which I seem never to tire—are, "Heaven," and "The Holy Spirit." In the former he spoke of a higher world to thousands who pass "the greater part of their time dreaming of this." In the latter *he yet speaketh,* urging upon Christian workers that it is not by might . . . nor by power . . . "but by my Spirit saith Jehovah of hosts."

Now all these, while very captivating, are merely scenes by the way.

*   *   *

We linger again, en route, to see how he built his sermons. Look! he carries note-books in his hip pocket! Every now and then he makes entries in a script that taxed even himself to read. (I *know.* I have read pages of his writing.) These notes were his lawful plunder; the things he begged, borrowed and kept. "I heard you preach from a text, and I went home and preached the same sermon to my people." When a great student of the Word came along, he "pumped him" (D. L.'s own idiom). "Give me something out of your heart: *your* best thought today: tell me something about Christ!"

Sometimes this got him into deep waters—as when he tried to appropriate Drummond.[1]

Mostly his first drafts were written out, practised in the hay-loft of his big Northfield barn, and first preached in Northfield. The writing was hurried; had no hammer marks on it. As he developed a sermon he used *Cruden's Concordance,* a topical text-book, and of course "read what Mr. Spurgeon had to say on the text." Then a big yellow manila envelope housed the first draft, and became a hopper into which he dropped clippings, notes and whatnots as the years went by. When a sermon was to be repeated he registered the date and place (plenty of such notations!), and then selected those materials from the supercharged envelope as most appealed to him at the time.

But remember, all the foregoing is purely secondary in this chapter!

*   *   *

We observe also, in passing, that his language is plain Anglo-Saxon, simple as his Franklin County hills, fiery with moral passion, impatient of complicated thoughts that lifted their heads above the level of common sense, making of him a Yankee Cobett, Bishop of Barns and Fields. The brooks of Spurgeon's boyhood sang and rippled through his three thousand sermons, but Moody was too much rushed with emergent things to tell us how lovely were the flowering laurels on Little Hemlock, or how alluring the river looked from the Great Meadow.

[1]See *Sowing and Reaping,* page 13.

Yet if he had no time to tell us about the organ tones of wood thrushes, he did discover practical lessons in milking cows regularly, and in cutting away apple-tree suckers. If he was silent about the purple patches shifting on Brattleboro's snows, he had plenty to say about poor corn-hoeing resembling inattentive Scripture reading ("one had to set a mark to tell where he left off") or the folly of pumping water for the cows without priming the pump. "It was easy to tell boarders from members of the family, when they sat down to dinner"—good wholesome Yankee wit unvexed with the subtleties of Sidney Smith.

Still, *mirabile dictu,* these commonplaces got your emotion all stirred up. You could hear God weeping over the Prodigal, as he told the story of Betsey's tears when run-away Isaiah came home again to Northfield. Your own soul trembled as he tolled the year-count of the church-bell for funeral services. You were melted like wax under his war stories; your heart cried with joy at a fresh view of Calvary's cross when he told of the back-firing he saw in early Illinois days, as men strove to escape the red ruin of prairie fires—"Calvary is the one safe place to abide: God's wrath has already burned over there!"

✓ Yes, you were moved to tears; he wanted you to be: "I tell stories to make the heart tender, and while it's tender, I sink the truth in!" Somebody said "he wasn't logical." Perhaps not, but his *emotional* sequence made logic look like a country cousin. And his contagious certainty that in Christ "the future is everything, the past nothing," made one glad to lose a schoolmarm's sensitiveness as to mere grammar.

Anyone reading Moody's sermons today, even in the Colportage Library, is at a loss to understand how they had such power. Remember, you are not really reading *his* sermons: you are following a *revision*, edited by his friends. Get a contemporary newspaper report, such as the New York *Tribune's*; where his "aints" and "taints" and "have gots" are faithfully set down; also the reaction of the crowds. Lo, you feel the revival starting afresh right in the privacy of your library. And another reason for disappointment in his printed sermons, *Moody's preaching was chiefly his personality-Bush Aglow!*

*   *   *

But it is time we regard the summum bonum. There is always peril living with the incidental. Thereby men who desire to imitate Moody settle on *casual*, rather than *causal* singularities. Just as they did in the case of John A. Broadus, who talked through his nose, or Charles R. Brown, who preaches with his thumbs in his pants' pockets.

*   *   *

Definitely, in 1871, a mysterious Quality lighted up Moody's personality: "he was transfigured before them." In no item was this whiteness of light more palpable than in his preaching. Other words cannot set forth in a phrase the reason for this auroral quality save those in The Thesaurus of Heaven—*he began making full proof of his ministry by preaching the Word!*

Now any inference whatever that Mr. Average Clergymen *does not* preach the Word touches his sciatic nerve. "Doesn't he spend hours on the works of Bible scholars? and doesn't he ransack libraries for sermonic filigree? Absurd!" Yet the stubborn fact remains that Bible preaching is mournfully scarce. The reasons?

Well, large platoons of preachers have retreated to Maxim Preaching. This makes dominies "amiable sophomores on a quest for truth." The "great thoughts" they glean from wide reading keep their souls in a sort of hectic spiritual flush. Their sermons are structures, to which a text is superficially attached—"Folks are accustomed to it, you know." References to the text are in effect mild surprises—that men living prior to V-eights had such discernment! "This old writer practically said the thing that I am saying; or at least it was nearly like it."

But Maxim Preaching is a thousand leagues from preaching the Word. It is a queer combination of attractive vagueness and pungency; "a statement of obviously practicable commonplaces in a manner not objectionably vigorous." It aims to start men putting things over with a bang, without worrying them with a sense of restraint. Maxim clergymen are almost sure to burn up before they give any light; they are, to quote another delightful maximeer, Bugs Bear, "Boobs in the woods, not sure where they are going, but blithesomely on their way."

Of course, Moody's early failure was not of *that* origin. Happily, he didn't know enough. His defects, reflected by another innumerable company, lay just here: Though he loved the Bible, "believed in it from back to back," yet, in sermonizing, he took a text, then promptly began fishing his own experience and consciousness for subject-matter. Which in the long last is a more intimate form of Maxim Preaching.

*   *   *

No attempt should be made to give a definition of "preaching the Word," unless we use the Word itself. Therein we are given to understand that men who preach the Word impress others at once that "the Word is very close to them, in their hearts and in their mouths, that is the Word which they preach." To such the sum of wisdom is simply and only "the Word of Christ, richly indwelling." They search the Testament in all things, enduring the charge of fogydom by people who turn their ears away from Bible statement. They know full well that intervals will come, again and again, when humanity, afflicted with itching ears, will be irritated by sound doctrine, heaping to themselves teachers after their own lusts, turning their ears from the Truth to fables! Nevertheless Word preachers are ready to endure such afflictions; the celestial credentials for their evangelism are not to be had from Monthly Maximeers; they find their sanctions in "The Law and the Testimony."

*   *   *

Moody faced the critical problem of becoming a genuine preacher of the Word. He quickly saw that it is *one* thing to *believe* the Bible, quite another to use it exclusively for framing material. Then his dismay arose, to find that human resolution failed to help him make the changes. He saw that a minister's sermonic nature must be born again, even as his soul. That even he, D. L. M., who had the first fruits of the Spirit, had spent weary months groaning within himself trying to reform his technique, when his real need was the *redemption* of his homiletical nature.

And, finally, that all this was just as much a charism as regeneration!

*   *   *

Following that New York November night in 1871, he had no further need to strive after being a Bible preacher: there was a far more elemental concern of which Bible preaching was simply a byproduct. His chief objective now was to walk in the Spirit: thereupon his sermons automatically held to the Word.

He then discovered that he did not need to throw away his precious personal experiences; they were now sanctified by the Word. But he noted that these secular manikins no longer posed as princes; they were humble servants. He filled his quiver with "newly baptized arrows." And he noted with chastened joy that his shafts, *after* they became Pauline, slew their tens of thousands; while in their Saulic condition they had simply an impotent fury.

His sermons now glowed with the power of the Burning Bush. Full-orbed truths of God, falling in quick succession from his lips with telling power, attracted millions of hearers, drawn from every walk of life: not the humble alone but equally those from the highest ranks. Jessie McKinnon speaks for the latter:

> "His preaching stirs my soul to its depths, touches every worthy spring of action,-gratitude to God, love and sympathy towards man, and everything in my nature between these two powers."

Toward the end of his life it lay heavily on his heart to admonish the ministry to "preach the Word!" On the twenty-seventh day of March, 1899, more than twenty-five hundred people filled the old First Congregational Church of San Francisco. Moody's deep concern over tomorrow's Zion kept breaking through. Once he censured the laity for "believing all that might come from the lips of an eloquent pulpiteer, without referring to the Word to see if it was God's message or only the fancy of an unregenerate mind."

Then he turned appealingly to the scores of Northern California ministers: "Don't be deceived. The coming preacher will be the one who takes the Word of God and makes it plain to the people. That man will have a hearing! The Bible and the Cross have power to draw, but a moral essay, never! I'm sick and tired of their essay-preaching. Will Bible preaching ever fail? No, a thousand times, No!

Highly cultured people ask me in surprise if there are those who really believe the Bible—*Well, I guess so!* If the minister who stands in the pulpit from week to week is *full of the Bible and the Holy Ghost,* people will be sitting in the aisles and crowding every available space, just as they are in this building today!"[2]

We turn to another San Francisco episode. It is the year 1881. The clerk of an ornate hotel on Market Street handed Moody a letter from England, just as he was to be driven in a cab to the old pavilion (hard by the site of the present City Hall). January rains had fallen for several days in a steady downpour; but the meetings had not suffered in the least. Everybody attended, from the Battered of the Barbary Coast to the young giants shaping California's new institutions.

Moody opened the letter; then turned on his heel, and hurried back to his room. Like Joseph, he wanted where to weep. His dear friend Harry Moorhouse had died at thirty-nine, just before Christmas! He walked over to the window, gazed upon the solid ranks of people moving from all directions toward the pavilion. Then he laughed, in his tears, as memory brought back certain words; words the Valorous Little Stephen had said to him long, long ago:

> "Moody, you're sailing on the wrong tack! If you will change your course, and learn to preach God's words instead of your own, *He will make you a great power!*"

[2]*The Examiner,* San Francisco, 3/28/1899, Washburne Collection.

XIX
HE SETS UP AN INQUISITION OF GRACE

Let no sincere Christian lightly pass over that certain engine of war which Pilgrim unfailingly employed in his final assault on man-soul. Having watched the walls fall through Faith's shouting, he esteemed it folly to move hastily away, thus leaving the Stricken Citizens of Vanity Fair to unfruitful confusion. Lo, he then marched straight into his conquest, promptly set up, without so much as an hour's delay, an Inquisition of Grace. Thereby, he and his fellow soldiers, with love in their hearts and light in their faces, did strictly inquire of each traitor, separately and with unhurried patience, for what reason he had fallen into rebellion against the King. Then each separate one had the reconciling message taught him, in the form best suited to his need and state of mind,–"God is all love, and has Himself atoned for our wicked rebellion through His anguish on the Tree." And when the heart of the trembling sinner came to that "willingness of the day of His power," Pilgrim established a mighty garrison in it from the Word of the King. And thus, thereby, the rebellious ones never again fell into defiance, nor did they ever cease to love the King.–*Sketch Book.*

HE SETS UP AN INQUISITION OF GRACE

There is a crowning event in the experience of a seeking sinner which, like the seal on a deed, establishes him in the grace of God, in all perpetuity. The New Testament calls it, "purpose of heart to cleave unto the Lord" (Acts 11:23). The context saves us from esteeming this "purpose of heart" to be mere human resolution toward divine loyalty; plainly, it is an utter casting of self upon Sufficient Grace. Rarely does this establishment take place *during* a preaching-service. Public meetings seldom do more than reduce a sinner's defences, and bring him to penitence. It is absolutely necessary *after* he comes into this frame to take him aside from the crowd for *specialized* care.

It is tragically uncertain that any man, being only awakened, can enter the rest of faith, unless there is "some man to guide him." It is Heaven's highest strategy, while the burden is still upon the sinner, to have a Spirit-filled Phillip come up, sit with him, open his mouth, and beginning at the point of awakened interest, preach unto him Jesus (Acts 8:31-37).

This kind of work is positively like creating life. Therefore it demands that Phillip shall strive toward the highest skill and wisdom, and be thoroughly under Guidance. He is the agent through whom Stricken Sinner is transmuted into Sturdy Saint.

The church of today has fallen into a fatal assumption-begotten either of ignorance or indolence, or both-namely, that a man who "lifts his hand or comes forward" is therefore established in grace. Thus our fellowships today are filled with people who "lack assurance"; we failed *them* in a crisis hour, and *they* retaliate by constantly failing the church in her crises hours. Once again we must return to this permanent attitude: to be *sure* that men savingly know Jesus, every inquirer must have a personal interview, unhurried and Guided. "Now *when the congregation was broken up,* many of the Jews and religious proselytes followed Paul and Barnabas: who, speaking to them, persuaded them to *continue in the grace of God!*" (Acts 13:43).

Call it by whatever name you may, Moody's Inquiry Room must be reestablished. And whatever name it may receive, the general specifications remain the same:

> It functions *immediately* after a gospel service: the workers, Spirit-led, deal unhurriedly with individuals; deal with them from the Word of God; wait, watch, secretly pray, patiently maneuver until Saving Faith arrives.

To use Moody's own words, "Continue patiently with one soul until it is on the Rock, till it sees the truth as God gives it. . . The other night I saw workers waiting a minute or two with one and then going on to another. Wait patiently! Ply them with God's Word; and think, oh! think, what it is to win a soul for Christ, and don't grudge the time spent on one person!"

Moody regarded the Inquiry Room as the polished shaft in his evangelical quiver. The swelling records of his days and nights of evangelism fairly bristle with references to the Inquiry Room. But we've almost lost our knowledge of it. That shelf in the church library made to hold such books is practically empty. There is a dust print showing where a little treatise once stood—Moody and Whittle, *Inquiry Meetings*—but I've failed to find a single copy, after world advertising. Incredible, that all the Moody writers have passed over his Inquisition of Grace with mere casual reference! All save one; and he, the most poorly equipped to undertake it.

*   *   *

The Inquiry Room must not be confused with Moody's "evangelical conviction." The latter was a permanent conviction that all Christian labor should have but one end in view, the salvation of the lost. To this he was committed from the beginning. As early as February, 1862, he emphatically stated, in the conference of a Christian relief committee aboard a steamer bound for the battlefield of Fort Donelson: "The very first business in every case is to find out if the sick or dying man is a child of God. If so, it is not necessary to spend much time on him; other organizations exist to look after his physical needs. If the man is *not* a Christian he is to be pointed at once to the Saviour."

Robert Collyer, pastor of a Chicago Unitarian

church, was nettled: "The *first* thing to do for these poor fellows is to administer whiskey, brandy, or milk punch. Brace up their nerves! What! are we to talk to our dying heroes, who have gone forth to save our flag, about thieves on the cross?"

Which sally was good for a big round of applause. But as it was quieting down, Moody gave the coup de grâce with a crisp statement: "I thank God I have never got *patriotism* mixed up with *piety!*"

This gospel immediacy runs straight through his utterances to the end: "His ultimate aim was to put soul-saving into every effort." "In this he was confirmed by war experience, where he was obliged to urge his hearers to accept immediate salvation." "He never would forgive himself that the night of the Chicago fire he slurred over the invitation, told them to think it over a week: it was such a dreadful lesson, brooding over those people who never came together again." "Even the relief of the poor was not so much for body comfort as soul salvation."

*   *   *

But the *Inquiry Room* was something entirely over and above gospel immediacy. It was one thing to urge acceptance of Christ in every service; it was a totally different thing to take men roused by such appeals; one by one, and see that "they got on the ark." The gospel appeal made a man ready to take salvation; the gospel clinic showed him how to do it—and made sure that he did! It was pure folly to permit any delay between roused interest and effectual treatment: "Don't say, 'If any are concerned

I will be glad to see them Friday night.' Deal with them *that night,* before the devil snatches away the seed." Permanent results were reserved to the after-meetings: "No use trying to make a lasting effect upon masses of people; put every effort on the individual. I knew a stupid minister who said that if anyone *might* be interested, the *session* would meet him. Might as well have asked him to go before a justice of the peace! If you want to get to an awakened soul, make it easy for him to see you alone."

*   *   *

Historically, the first influence that led Moody to set up the Inquiry Room was a statement made to him, while still a boy, by his old grandfather, Luther Holton:[1] "In my day there was a great revival and every one came to the anxious bench, and *were talked to*; but now they don't do so, and I don't believe it is the work of God." In 1859 he began developing the Inquiry Room in his general Sunday school work. He quickly abandoned the Anxious Bench form; public conditions were too distracting; pressure too high. The awakened ones were taken to separate rooms to secure maximum privacy. By 1868 his method was highly advanced and a permanent climax of his Chicago church work. By 1873 the technique was so fully developed that according to Ian Maclaren its operation in the Edinburg meetings was "the infirmary in which Drummond learned Spiritual Diagnosis."

[1] Statement reported by the New York *Tribune,* 1876.

The psychological and spiritual principle that undergirded the Inquiry Room was brilliantly stated by Henry C. Mabie, at one time corresponding secretary of the American Baptist Foreign Mission Society.[2] When Mabie was a young student in Chicago he was profoundly influenced by Moody. Moody's ideals, sowed in the boy's heart, came to a full harvest during a spiritual crisis in 1884, "reshaping his whole career." Through the technique of the Inquiry Room, Mabie came to know and to practise the priceless truth that,

> "Effective faith involves a decisive act of the will to some *present* measure of spiritual light. This will-act, more than theoretic belief in truth as a system of intellectual proportions, is the chief element in 'belief of the heart unto righteousness.' And the highest work we can ever do for another soul is to afford incentive to immediately treat the measure of truth it *already* knows as a reality, and so to act upon it."

*   *   *

Let us view Moody's Inquiry Room in its chief aspects. Generally, it "straightway" followed a gospel service. (Though sometimes, *without a gospel service,* people came in response to advertisements; and sometimes interest became so deep that it ran two full days a week.) A large room was prepared for use immediately following the sermon, together with as many side rooms as possible. (*"Prepared"*

---

[2] Read his *Method in Soul-Winning;* a classic.

meant heated, ventilated, set in order.) Generally, the workers came in first; were admonished; then Moody said, "Now distribute yourselves; I am going to call in the inquirers." The inquirers entered, commonly two hundred, sometimes a thousand. It should be said that Moody desired to get people into his Inquisition of Grace in any state of mind: "It's a place for sowing seed as well as gathering grain."

Moody then spoke to the inquirers, en masse, tenderly, pointedly, briefly; spoke with fluent scriptural accuracy upon such topics as "receive," "believe," "trust," "take," so simply a child could understand. He then attempted to sift them into groups: the deeply anxious; those lacking assurance; and so on. Thereafter, they broke up for private interview, preferably in private rooms; if not, in quiet groups in the big room.

"One at a time" was the rule; never violated unless they were thronged; "one at a time was sensible: there was a right remedy for each: a good doctor didn't give cod-liver oil for all complaints." This scientific investigation of the individual brought to Drummond much amazement; he saw that hundreds of church-members were lacking in assurance, tragically deficient in practical knowledge as to the new birth. Jessie McKinnon mentioned "the surprise of sitting beside an inquirer whom we had surely thought to be a Christian already." You see these unhappy members had been taken for granted, their deepest need ignored when they "joined the church."

Moody insisted that workers in the Inquiry Room

must strive for thorough equipment; be approved in character; certain of their own salvation.

"We won't have them if their records are not clean; *difficult to enforce, but I've done* it many a time; if a man isn't right, I go to him, and insist he straighten out his life before we want him; if he gets angry that settles it,-shows he is not right: but if he breaks down,-that's different!"

"Workers must be skillful in discernment; able to perceive at once different classes and deal accordingly. Some inquirers lack assurance; some are backsliders; some shackled by gross sins; some need to have props, as moral excellence, knocked out; some with excuses; cranks, spiritualists, infidels and smart Alecs; some under conviction; some can be brought under conviction."

"Hear closely the difficulties of each; plead with the Spirit for just the right word. In every case always use your Bible; don't trust to memory; make the person read for himself. *And don't argue!* Get him at last on his knees: you may need to talk two hours: *but don't get him on his knees until he is ready!*"[3]

D. L., Emma, and Sankey were the most skillful of all life-changers. It is well to study them in action. Their interest at once was riveted to the inquirers: "If notable strangers were introduced to

---

[3]Quotations in this chapter a mosaic from a hundred books; too many for detailed reference.

Moody at the end of the meetings, he brushed conventional courtesies aside and darted off in a moment to awakened souls." They were marked by a "habitual, powerful realization of the value of a soul." "It was beautiful to see them keep themselves out of sight, pointing to Jesus only."

And the Bible was their chief dependence.

> "They seemed to pass over themselves as instruments, and with the open Bible, to fix on the truths of God, and the power of the Spirit." "Moody speaks to inquirers with an open Bible in his hands, fixing them down to the Word of God, and anchoring their souls on the Living Rock." . . "A man cannot be convicted by any means save *The Holy Spirit working through the Word*: he may know he's a great sinner, but the Holy Spirit must bring conviction." "They kept at a case an hour, or two, or three! . . talking the inquirers out of self and into Christ."

> *"And, it was almost invariably in the end, a portion of God's Word, either with or without explanation that brought them into the light!"*

*　　*　　*

Time fails to furnish an inventory of the "established" souls who came into the Kingdom by way of the Inquisition of Grace; thousands like Studd. Impossible to tabulate the energy devoted by workers in Moody's day. Some statistician says that Moody himself prayed with seventy-five thousand. No wonder the church took hold, and "there were giants."

We must set it up again. Pay the full price of becoming Evangelical Psychographers. Know that the church cannot be stocked anew with robust Christians until we do! This is the only way to produce Christians knowing whom they have believed, and thereby serving their generation by the will of God. This type of emphasis can never be outmoded. It is effort bringing forth fruit a hundredfold; and yielding joy ahead of any other Christian activity. Baxter said, it was like "eating angel's bread to hear the cry of conviction, then to see the joy of reconciliation." Never mind if our inert age objects. They did in Moody's day. A heckling Scotch dominie shouted, "I dinna believe in disturbing holy impressions! Ye don't sow seed, then dig it up to see if it has sprouted!" To which Moody replied, amid a storm of applause, *Perhaps not: but the farmers all harrow it in after it's sowed!* We must set it up anew–if we are to meet the crisis of the age through God's uniform method of dealing with nations,–a great awakening. We must seek that grace which Jessie McKinnon set forth in a notable description of Moody:

> "Dear hard worker! and all for the love of souls! What Christian could look unmoved on him going on thus, night after night, watching at every turn, looking after every one, with constant demands on him . . . in nerve and patience, quiet, calm, unperturbed! How could we help loving him! Once while waiting I had the chance of seeing (and how I was touched by it!) his tender-

ness of heart and manner towards the anxious. I did not see her face (the one with whom he was dealing) but his was towards me. *How full of earnest tender compassion! his whole face and attitude were full of beseechings, as an ambassador of Christ.*

"Happy undignified work! What an honor and I can never be thankful enough that I was allowed to have a share in it!"

THE HOUSES OF PILGRIM'S TROWEL

Auditorium, Moody Memorial Church, Chicago, Illinois

(Courtesy Henry Allan Ironside, Pastor)
Membership, 1936, 3,986. Capacity, 4,040

The Moody Bible Institute, Chicago, Illinois

(Courtesy Will H. Houghton. President.) Thirty-eight buildings; towers of radio station WMBI, several miles away, "foreshortened" into picture

Enrolment, 1936: Day School, 806; Evening School, 952; Correspondence School, 9,700.

Total, 1936–11,458

Northfield Seminary, Northfield, Massachusetts

Enrolment, 1936, 548

Mount Hermon School for Boys, Northfield, Massachusetts

Enrolment, 1936, 583

XX
PILGRIM TAKES UP A TROWEL
(1879-1899)

Now, Pilgrim rose up each morning, a great while before day, that he might keep trysts with his King. Lo, he felt deep need to do this: for if he came to such a pother in caring for the King's Business, that no time remained to gaze upon the King's Face, the joy of his salvation did fade away. Moreover, these trysts did bring him another large blessing: Thereby he was able to discern just when the King desired him to go into the Next Towns. (Mark 1:35-38.)

During these hours apart, the Lord did open his mind to see that the Interpreter's House must be put in charge of Mr. Great Heart, rather than Mr. Great Head. It was naught but high treason to set the souls of the Young Redeemed under the tutelage of men who did neither know nor believe that the beginning of Wisdom was the fear of Jehovah. He perceived, therefore, that the Next Towns his Lord desired him to occupy were Commonschool and Jordanseminary.

So he took his father's trowel and built three great houses, one for young damsels; one for young yeomen, and one for young prophets. And he saw it was good; a way was opened for an army of yeomen and prophets, having Head Knowledge mated to Heart Wisdom.

Now he bound together the foundation walls of each of these three houses with a Book, a Precious Corner Stone. And he prayed no man might ever in folly assay to remove it; for if they did,——!—*Sketch Book.*

PILGRIM TAKES UP A TROWEL
(1879-1899)

When Zion begins to "multiply a thousandfold" she immediately faces up to the necessity of establishing her own institutions of education. She understands that though mental culture is somewhat neutral it does make a difference of east-west width as to what sort of man sits in the professor's chair. It is entirely irrelevant to compare the mere teaching skill of Professor Arrant Doubter and Professor Humble Believer. Either may do equally well, from Home Economics to Astral Dynamics. But the critical influences that shape the life of Mr. Young Student arise far more from the evangelical quality of the teacher's life than from the technical excellence of his pedagogy. Inescapable correlates of this truth run clear down to the thesis, "It is far better to provide the Sons and Daughters of Zion with an admittedly inferior training under men of faith than a brilliant superficiality under unbelievers."

Here we observe the grim necessity that forced Moody to become an educator. During the British revival, when he sensed an awakening church, he also discerned the folly of turning over the Lord's children to the Lord's enemies. The primary motivation behind his establishment of the vast Moody Institutions was a keen insight into this truth. A mere humanitarian desire to put culture within the

reach of handicapped youth did not interest him at all, as
we see in his Northfield Seminary apologetic:

> "You know, the Lord laid it upon my heart to
> organize a school for young women in the humbler
> walks of life to get a *Christian* education . . . I hope
> it may be a power in bringing souls to Christ,"

and at Mount Hermon:

> "It undertakes to furnish for earnest Christian
> young men opportunities to secure a better
> preparation . . . men diligent in spirit, serving
> the Lord."

And he saw to it that a Bible was placed in the corner-
stone of every major building.

His mind was practically made up when he returned to
America, August 14, 1875, convinced by what Charles
Haddon Spurgeon had shown him, and confirmed by the
founding of the "Calico College" (Wellesley) of his friend,
Henry F. Durant, in 1875, His plans matured during the
mighty revivals in American cities during the three years
1876-1878. Within four years of his return to America, he
was laying the corner-stone of the first edifice of the giant
Moody system of today.

There was a circumstance of highest dramatic
interest in the laying of that first corner-stone, spring
of 1879. A crowd was gathered about the founda-

tions of the building-to-be, in the hundred-acre plot just above Northfield recently acquired by Moody—"bare sandy hillocks, useless even for pastureland." Moody wielded a battered old trowel, whose hickory handle was checked from end to end, while on the trestle board, ignored, lay a new silver trowel.

The old trowel had been the property of his father and grandfather before him. Mrs. Elizabeth Moody Washburne told her daughter Miriam Elim the story, "a thousand times": "The heartless couple Mr. and Mrs. Scrooge came up to the Homestead in the summer of 1844 to foreclose on the note given by the dead father. They took practically every movable thing; but there was one thing they didn't get; the children hid their father's masonic tools under a board in the attic. Here, like Manna in the Ark they remained until"—until that day when D. L., now a man of forty-two, entering a new area of life, went into the attic, knelt in prayer, then moved the secret panel and grasped his father's trowel. From now on he was to serve God as evangelist *and* builder. "With one of his hands he wrought on the wall, and with the other held a sword." What an appropriate thing to take up his own father's trowel just where death had struck it from his grasp on that far-away afternoon!

Sankey, though unaware of the above story, supplies the finishing detail: "Mr. Moody was laying the corner-stone . . . his friends had secured a silver trowel . . . but he refused to use it . . . in the garret he had gotten his father's old trowel with which he had earned bread for his family . . . 'You may keep the silver trowel,' he said, 'this one is good enough for me!'"

*   *   *

Moody's assumption of the trowel, however, really began with the institution dearest to his heart, the nurturing mother of all the rest, the institution in which his membership continued until his death, the Moody Memorial Church. His building activities in connection with the church rested, in 1876, upon the dedication of the edifice at Chicago Avenue and La Salle Street. But the very momentum of his ideals, enlisting the labors of thousands of others, is to be observed in the church's history since his death.

The Chicago Avenue Church building was taken over by the vigorous child of the church, the Moody Bible Institute, in 1915. The church then rented a lot at North Avenue, Clarke and La Salle Streets, erected a five-thousand-capacity, barn-like tabernacle, at an expense of $23,000; then in 1917 purchased the lot for $265,000. In the week of November 8, 1925, the present simple, age-abiding structure was dedicated: a million-dollar building of which all Christendom may be proud.

It is an edifice impressive in every detail. The vast auditorium, "made to hear in and to see in," has four thousand forty seats, not one of which is vexed by pillar, columns or obstruction. The spacious Bible school suite provides for twenty-five hundred pupils. The architects—influenced by certain Romanesque, Italian churches, and also by St. Sophia in Constantinople-dreamed out an edifice apparently made for the people. And sure enough the people attend. Go and see for yourself any Sunday from bitter February to burning August.

What a mighty church it is! Of its 3,986 members,[1] one hundred and twelve are in world-wide missionary service, sixty of whom are supported entirely by the church, at a yearly cost of forty thousand dollars. The Bible school has an enrolment of 1,751.

Great in every particular, in lay evangelism, youth movements, city missions; in its pastoral succession -J. H. Harwood, W. J. Erdman, C. N. Morton, George C. Needham, Charles A. Blanchard, Charles F. Goss, F. B. Hyde, R. A. Torrey, A. C. Dixon, E. Y. Wooley, Paul Rader, P. W. Philpott and H. A. Ironside. And greatest of all in its fire of perennial revival.

But it faces centennial year with a burdensome debt of $250,000, due to unfortunate circumstances beyond its control. Chicago enforced an eighteen-foot widening of La Salle Street which ran up the costs of adjustment in the sum of $239,000. This, together with depression and pledge-shrinkage, saddled upon the church the debt just mentioned.

No more appropriate gesture of love for Moody, for Moody's most beloved institution, and Moody's Lord, could be made by the hundreds of thousands of interested people throughout the world than fully to release this burden. Let a flood of subscriptions

[1]Statistics as of January 1, 1936, furnished by Charles Augustin Porter, Associate Pastor.

come in from all over the world! So small a sum as one dollar will bring to the donor a centennial certificate. One of these certificates, signed by Pastor H. A. Ironside, is framed and hanging in my study Beside the Golden Gate; a cherished possession.

*   *   *

It is a far cry from November 1, 1879, when Moody, impatient of delay, launched the Northfield Seminary in his own home, to the strength of the present institution. The school began with twenty-five girls, on a barren pasture; today there are five hundred and forty-eight, on a campus of Cambridge beauty. After fifty-six years a herd of noble edifices and sturdy young trees are patterned out on the hills. Some of the buildings were financed by hymn-book royalties; at least one "sung up by Sankey"; others, the gifts of friends–Gould Hall, Kenarden Hall, Russell Sage Memorial Chapel, Palmer Hall, Margaret Olivia Hall, Talcott Library, the Auditorium, East Hall. There's another great rambling multi-story frame building, The Northfield Inn, just south of the campus, on its own Del Monte grounds. It has a significant history. Moody erected the original unit so as to entertain "likely" visitors (likely to have money for the Northfield Seminary!).

Satellite to the Seminary are other enterprises launched by Moody: the Northfield Bible Conference (first call issued in 1880), where many of the world's greatest Christians have been heard in summer assemblies; the Missionary Conference; the College Students' Conference; the Girls' Conference; every one of which was launched to insure the indoctrination of men and women in training for Christian leadership.

And as a Bethel-center of it all, Round Top, that winsome little hill that has changed in the years from a barren knob to a forested knoll, beneath the shade of which lie the graves of two Revered Ones.

*   *   *

Mount Hermon, the school for boys, followed quickly on the heels of Northfield Seminary. Through the generous twenty-five-thousand-dollar gift of Hiram Camp, New Haven clock manufacturer, the school opened May 1, 1881. Two farms were purchased, making a tract of two hundred and seventy-five acres on the west bank of the Connecticut, four miles south of Northfield–just across the old turnpike from Mother Moody's birthplace. The first classes were held in the overhauled farm buildings; but exactly like Northfield Seminary, the following years have witnessed the addition of noble edifices, financed by hymn-book royalties and friends. The campus is of another type of beauty, a rugged grandeur quite up to California's Mendocino. The school began with one student; today there are five hundred and eighty-three.[2]

The two units are now jointly administered as the Northfield Schools, and as such constitute the largest private secondary school in the United States. Both,

[2]Statistics of the Northfield Schools, furnished by Samuel E. Walker, of Northfield, nephew of D. L. M.; and Ethel Gladwin, Alumnæ Office Assistant.

from inception, have insisted on student participation in farm and home duties, and have been kept within reach of thousands by low fees. The total number of students to date, in both units, has been 26,229 (Northfield Seminary 11,076; Mount Hermon, 15,153). Many of these students have come to world fame; thousands are the Salt of the earth as mothers, wives, fathers, husbands-citizens. Deeply impressive is it to look in on the high type of business administration, and to note how every boy and girl is followed throughout life. This very week I had a letter from Northfield asking about a former student. She is a Mother in Israel now; trained, consecrated, and at the age of seventy-four teaching a class of girls in my San Francisco church. She was one of Moody's first five students-Mrs. Clara White Alder.

*   *   *

The Moody Bible Institute of Chicago does not occupy a sylvan campus, nor does it have ornate edifices. A first glance at the thirty-eight brick buildings, herded together in the area of a city block, is disappointing, especially if it's the dead o'summer. But go into the concrete desert, even with Chicago's sultry July sun glaring down, and you are gripped by the seven-league tempo of life,- the laughter of hastening groups of youth, the summer cadence of pianos through open windows, the shuffling of hundreds of feet over wooden floors, the bursts of gospel music. Six buildings of the thirty-eight will rise in your estimate-the Original Building, the Audito-

rium (old Chicago Avenue Church edifice), Women's
Building, Men's Dormitory, Publication Building, and the
Office Annex, where sainted Doctor Gray, at the age of
eighty-four, kept office hours until a week before his death
on September 21, 1935. And they will tell you of a great
new Administration Building now in prospect.
Contemplating this rush of energy, we feel like saying,
with the discoverer of the Amazon's mouth, "This river
drains a continent!" Behind it lie fifty years of Titanic
activity, in a word, half a century of devotion to one Book.
In that period it has centered, for a student's interval, the
lives of tens of thousands of men and women. For sheer,
spectacular gianthood, the Bible Institute is the Mt.
Everest of the Moody Institutions and, for that matter,
unique in the history of Christianity.

One quickly forgets the dismal bricks and becomes
fascinated with the Talus stride-whether he approves of it
or not. As one who loves each Moody institution, who
esteems them a most impressive achievement of Christian
faith, I risk a storm of argument in stating: *The Bible
Institute incarnates more fully than any of the others, Moody's
unique personality, dynamic power, great purposes, and,
deathless devotion to the Book.*

It is the best of institutions-it is the worst
of institutions. It is the best of institutions to
thousands who have found grace in the classrooms,
under fervid instructors; to thousands who have
received life eternal through its evangels; and to
thousands who, by reason of the literature flooding
from its presses, see in it a power for faith in the last days.

It is the worst of institutions to thousands who esteem it a perilous educational shortcut; to thousands who deprecate excess evangelical warmth; and to thousands who, at odds with the doctrine of an inspired Bible, are offended by the Institute's "Bibliolatry."

It is difficult exactly to classify the Institute. Certainly it is not a theological seminary; and certainly the work is of too high a grade to be dismissed as a mere "Bible institute," Perhaps the cleverest half-truth discrimination is this that we heard in Chicago last summer: "Men go to seminaries in order to *get* a church; they come to Moody in order to *keep* it."

Do not forget that the development of Moody Bible Institute is a mosaic, the separate units representing the lives and labors of a host of Great Hearts. And the inlaying which began under the personality of Moody, while he lived, continued under his ideals after his death. The devotion of Emeline E. Dryer, Reuben Archer Torrey, James Martin Gray, and a host of equally dedicated men and women, constitutes the Alpha-Omega design laid down by "the Apt to Teach." The humble background against which the loveliness of the pattern is exhibited was provided by the self-effacement of a legion of willing Amaziahs, like Mrs. Cyrus H. McCormick, John V. Farwell and Henry P. Crowell.

Evidently the Institute considers its birthday to be February, 1886. At that time it was resolved to regiment an already vigorous movement under the name, "The Chicago Evangelization Society." But

we must not lose sight of the heroic pioneering of
Emeline E. Dryer, years before 1886. Her heart and mind
were captured as early as 1872 by the fiery convictions of
her young lay pastor, D. L. M. He was certain that neither
Chicago nor America, nor the world, could be roused for
God unless thousands of common people were trained
and sent out "to preach the Word." Could he be silent in
this matter, or give it up? No! a thousand times, No!

In 1882 she resigned her office as dean of women at the
Illinois State Normal College in order to devote her full
time to Moody's scheme of training evangelical workers.
For fourteen years prior to 1886 she headed up Bible
teaching among women, training of Bible readers and city
missionaries, first "in the ashes" around the North Side
Tabernacle, and finally in the Chicago Avenue Church.

This "indomitable little lady" made a trip to
New York in February, 1876, while Moody was in
the Hippodrome meetings, to urge upon him the securing
of buildings wherein Bible workers could live while
they were being trained. Her heart was set on several
"brick dumps" adjacent to the Chicago Avenue Church
(little did she dream she was about to force the church
off that corner!). In October, 1876, Moody, while
holding meetings in the Chicago Tabernacle, approved,
and the buildings were rented. The movement at
once exhibited "an annoying vitality"; all over Chicago
it spread in tents, churches, empty buildings. By the
year 1885, the "amorphus thing" was clamoring for
organization. Moody, en route to a southern revival, con-

ferred with the aggressive leaders, and said in effect, "No organization until you have $250,000 in cash!" And in six months they had it.

On January 22, 1886, Moody delivered his historic address in the Chicago Avenue Church on "City Evangelization": "I believe we have got to have 'gap men,' men who are trained to fill the gap between the common people and the ministers. We are to raise up men and women who will be willing to lay their lives alongside of the laboring." This was followed by the formal decision, in February, 1886, to organize "The Chicago Evangelization Society."

In February, 1887, the name was changed to "The Bible Work Institute." Its "annoying vitality" became more marked. The annual Institute for Bible Study, usually held in May, was set for April, 1889, so as "to get Moody in attendance." At that time he capitulated to the idea of a Bible Institute in Chicago, and arranged the purchase of the lots adjoining the church. Three buildings were used as women's dormitories; the erection of one for men was begun.

Moody immediately (to use an appropriate western state expression) "rode herd" on a brilliant young Yale dominie, who had done post-graduate work in Leipzig and Erlangen, Reuben Archer Torrey. Before Torrey had time to think, he was "roped up"; and on September 26, 1889, "The Chicago Bible Institute" formally began, with him as superintendent.

For sixteen months preliminary financing was a

staggering difficulty. But the receipt of generous gifts, such as $10,000 from the Scotch Robert Dollar, Peter McKinnon, caused Moody to write McKinnon, "I feel as if now, should I be called away, the work will go on. . . I will always look on 1890 as the year I reached the top of the hill—and you helped me get there."

By the time of Moody's death, the physical equipment was worth nearly $400,000. Under the leadership of James Martin Gray, 1904-1935, the institution added building after building, until today there are thirty-eight, with a total value of $5,000,000. On November 1, 1934, the vigorous young Southern Baptist, with a Yankee background, Will H. Houghton, was called from the Calvary Baptist Church of New York to succeed Doctor Gray—just in time to plan the semi-centennial celebration of February, 1936. And now, with forty persons on the faculty and a little regiment of Bible teachers and evangelists in the Extension Department, there is more annoying vitality than ever! [3]

Statistics incident to the centennial observance are staggering. They show that to August 31, 1936, 19,785 have enrolled as resident day students; 17,219 as evening students; 83,257 as Correspondence School students; 9,469 in the Radio School of the Bible; making the incredible sum total of 129,730. The Correspondence School now enrolls 9,700.

[3]Bible Institute statistics, brought up to date, are edited by the author from letters and personal interviews with James Martin Gray, Will H. Houghton, Clarence H. Benson, William Norton, and Harold L. Lundquist. Valued help has also been received from Wilbur Moorehead Smith, Editor of *Peloubet's Notes*.

Satellite to the Institute is a group of enterprises, such as Radio Station WMBI; the Bible Institute Colportage Association, and its department, the Moody Missionary Book Funds; the Great Commission Prayer League; and the Evangelical Teacher Training Association. In addition to this, there is the All Bible Graded Series, not officially connected with the Institute, but produced under Dr. Clarence H. Benson and a group of workers, who are either of the faculty or graduates of the Christian Education Course.

All these enterprises are bewilderingly vast. The Colportage Association has published books in one hundred seventy-seven titles and six languages, totaling eleven million copies; one million hymn-books; and thirty-five million tracts. It employs five hundred part-time colporters. The Book Fund has "a national network" to take the gospel to the neglected—prisoners, pioneers, lumberjacks, navy gobs, mountaineers, orphans, army men and "Alphabetic camps."

*   *   *

Some Christian institutions of education exhibit a melancholy bias toward a steady decline from their original evangelical warmth, and an increasing emphasis upon mere intellectual excellence. But the process is so thoroughly subconscious that our Cultural Samsons warmly affirm primitive virtues, and set themselves to carry off Gaza's Gates, tragically unaware that God has departed from them. The mere name "Moody" cannot permanently guarantee

a single unit of the Moody suite, whether Institute or
Seminary. Already there are omens that demand
rethinking. Moody dreamed of a regimentation of his
several institutions, which today has practically
disappeared. He desired, as cap-sheaf function, that his
schools should work together in preparing young people
for world evangelization:

> "I want to take young persons at the age of
> sixteen to twenty, *to Northfield,* and give them a
> good English training, and when they prove
> themselves worthy, *to send them to Chicago.* And
> there they go on studying the Bible and working,
> and as fast as they can prove themselves good
> workmen, send them out to all lands. I am in hopes
> I will send out a thousand a year. *What the nation
> wants is not BIG men, but small men,-little in their
> own sight!-Nobodies! and then God will use them!"* [4]

[4]Source material, Washburne Collection.

XXI
THE SWORD AND THE TROWEL
(1879-1899)

Now Christiana was sorely troubled when she and Pilgrim started on their Progress, by reason of the strange fire in which Pilgrim moved. She perceived naught stood between him and destruction save youth's dwindling vigors. Then her eyes beheld a mystery. There came a day in which the human in him died out, and a Fire from on high flooded his being. Now, instead of *diminishing* his labors, he greatly *added* to them. Not only did he continue to wield Evangel's sword with his right hand, but he took up a trowel in his left, and powerfully wrought on Zion walls. Lo, while his exploits were greater than ever, *yet he himself seemed* always, now, at rest!

One day as they did walk together beside a Blue Sea of Syria, he told her of an aged man who formerly had much annoyed him.

"This aged person said to me, 'Young man, honor thou the Holy Ghost or thou shalt break down!' And I was angry. But he was right! My heart was troubled and I prayed: prayed, until there came the night when Third Heaven found me. . . Since then my soul has known the mystery of Moses' bush which burned with Fire,–*but was not consumed!*

"My dear, you know I was an older man before I was thirty, than I've ever been since!"–*Sketch Book.*

THE SWORD AND THE TROWEL
(1879-1899)

Love's labor of writing this book comes to an end with the world at Spring. It seems that a very great time has passed since the work began in early December. But I have eaten angels' bread and stood in the presence of the King. Regretfully, I am beginning to file away-forever, so far as I am concerned -the bulky research notations; regretfully, because this book has not woven half the skeins available. Such vivid colors, such fascinating detail! All of which must be denied a place because it does not step right along in developing the theme.

There is, for instance, my Biographical Year-Table, taking into account almost every month of Moody's life, which alone would outsize this volume. But a casual review of this Year-Table brings one face to face with a perennial mystery: "How can a man, years on end, *increase* his labors, carry a universe on his shoulder-as he did? How can one do it without breaking down? Yea, how can he do it, and yet *always seem at rest?*"

Looking over the Year-Table, one notes where the Furious Thirties are succeeded by the Quieter Forties and Fifties. But, the tempo never slackens; the "Christian output" increases. Now this book is concerned with making an inventory of Moody's increasingly large exploits only in so far as this fascinating theme is served, namely:

> When the Fire of God indwells our humble humanity, we have power to move with April freshness amidst boundless responsibilities: it is not *work* which destroys us: but *work in the flesh.*

The Broad Brim Gentlemen whom Spurgeon loved laughed at the fears of the Lord's servants who esteemed themselves apt to perish from overwork: "Something's amiss, good friends! There's naught so restorative and health-giving *as labor in the Lord!*"

Just read down that complicated Year-Table, recording Moody's busy life. Note how, at the age of forty-two, he added to his sword a trowel, "building on the wall with one of his hands and with the other holding a weapon" (Nehemiah 4:17, 18). And see that his health actually prospered under it. Ah, that is to get a vision of God's grace which He desires to give every one of His servants, the economy of which He setteth forth in a Flaming Bush, brilliant enough to light a desert, and yet not wasting away! *"And the bush was not consumed!"*

Moody's unfretted endurance is a mystery to men who have not read the third chapter of Exodus "with the understanding." Some tried to explain it on the ground that he could sleep instantly and soundly. They noted his practice of "forty winks." On railway trains, in horse-drawn vehicles, yea, even when a boresome person talked to him, he could "get away a few moments, then come right back fresh as a lark." Over and over he dozed off ten minutes before preaching; was awakened at the precise time, and began talking to the great multitude as with the dew of his youth. But, let no man forget, there is a wide difference between slumber, and *the sleep which the Lord doth give His beloved.*

The Year-Table shows that there was hardly a city of importance in America which Moody did not visit. In addition, two more revivals in England. And in the midst of it all a personal interest in his Chicago and Northfield institutions. Here is a brief sampling of these activities:

1879. Many weeks of meetings in various churches of Baltimore; meeting in Cleveland–and the setting up of his schools.

1880. Great meetings in St. Louis and San Francisco–and his schools and summer assemblies.

1881-1884. Second English revival, in the midst of which he made a trip to America to inspect his institutions.

1885-1890. Revivals all over the South: New Orleans, Houston, Richmond, etc.; in Canada; in Eastern United States–and his institutions, to which was added the Bible Institute.

1891. Third and last great English revival–and the financing of his growing schools.

1893. The Columbian Exposition Evangelistic Program, incredibly complicated–and his schools.

1894. Eleven revivals, in such cities as Washington, Toronto, Birmingham, Scranton–and, of course, his schools.

1895. Meetings in New York, Boston, Philadelphia, Worcester, etc.–and his schools.

1897. Meetings in Cincinnati, Chicago, Winnipeg, etc.–and his schools.

1898. Head of Y. M. C. A. Subcommittee on Evangelism, Spanish-American War. (At that juncture he crisply told the leadership that his work was "evangelism, not providing writing-paper!") Also meetings in Jersey City, Pittsburgh, Montreal, Denver, etc.–and his schools.

1899. Meetings in Phoenix, Tucson, San Diego, Santa Barbara, Los Angeles, San Francisco, Kansas City–his schools–and, the Gates of Glory.

* * *

Statistics of these meetings are bewildering. Someone asked, "How many souls have been saved under your preaching?" He said, "I'm glad I don't have to keep Gabriel's books." One writer affirms that he preached to over one hundred million people. A careful estimate on the basis of my Year-Table reveals that he spent almost ten thousand days and nights in meetings; a stupendous total, which, if put together, would make *a continuous revival over twenty-five years long.*

Last summer, in the quiet lobby of the Northfield Inn, we visited with one who went repeatedly to Northfield when Moody was alive. Of course he dreamed of those great Bible Conferences when, after the sessions, "We didn't stop to discuss the speakers or their messages; we went off into the woods to pray." It was well worth while in those days to get D. L. talking about how God sustains His servants in impossible labors by means of Divine Fire: "I once met a minister in London whose health became so poor he could only preach once a week. . . He got *freshly anointed*. . . Told me now he preached eight sermons a week . . . and he never had been so well!"

*   *   *

No attempt is made to relieve the impression that this chapter ends abruptly. Why keep the shuttles moving any longer on the little tapestry? We just put a finishing border on it by suggesting that men in the Will of God do not break down under His pressures; they know and live and labor and rest in the mystery of "My grace is sufficient,

> FOR MY STRENGTH IS MADE PERFECT IN WEAKNESS. MOST GLADLY THEREFORE WILL I RATHER GLORY IN MY INFIRMITIES, THAT THE POWER OF CHRIST MAY REST UPON ME."

THE COMMONER OF NORTHFIELD

"He Groweth Much Heavenward"

Dwight Lyman Moody at Fifty-five and the Main Street of Northfield

"My Human Best,
  Filled with the Holy Spirit."

XXII
He Groweth Much Heavenward

"His style is the same, but quieter. . . There has been a mellowing power at work, not all of nature. . . He is the same but quieter,—the same, but one feels he has grown much heavenward. . . The human in him has lessened in power and the heavenly has greatly advanced. . . Self, little seen before, is now far away, and out of ken."—*Jessie McKinnon.*

He Groweth Much Heavenward

There is a point at which the writing of biography ceases to be laborious and becomes a winging rapture of full creative flight. If the subject be a mail of Olympian endowments, one must guard against the flight lapsing into a stunting solo. This came perilously near happening in writing of Charles Haddon Spurgeon. So fully was I enamored of that multisided personality that the sane movement of strong emotion under sure control was at the point of breaking down into galloping panegyric. Deliverance arose from a spiritual experience, the like of which one never fully discusses . . . the saving check came as the aggrieved man of the broad brim seemed to be pleading, "Don't praise me, praise Him!"

Well, the rapture of flight in writing of Moody has never arisen from admiration of his genius. It is said respectfully, and in so saying Infinite Grace is magnified, Moody was essentially commonplace. For this, I thank God. No wonder my heart has found in the Commoner of Northfield a more powerful encouragement than in the Heir of the Puritans. It has come as a song in the night to find in D. L. sure proof that the loftiest achievement is merely "my human best, filled with the Holy Spirit."

Thus this midbook portrait is concerned in exhibiting Moody in his loftiest attainment, namely his so living that those who looked fixedly upon him saw no man, but Jesus only.

Mrs. Jessie McKinnon discerned in Moody the outworking of that process whereby men come to be no longer themselves, but Christ that liveth in them. And she stated in a woman's limpid prose:

> "Mr. Moody is among us again (October, 1881), and we are right glad to have him. He is the same simple, straightforward man we knew him to be in former years . . . the same, but quieter. We think he is quieter altogether-probably the difference that; eight years naturally makes in a man . . . so it strikes one at first, but we are not long beside him till we find there has been a mellowing power at work, not all of nature. He is the same, but quieter, *the same but one feels he has grown much heavenward* . . . the human in him has lessened in power, and the heavenly has greatly advanced . . . self, little seen before, is now far away and out of ken. . ."

I never look at the picture of mature Moody, mounted upon his beloved Northfield Main Street, without Mrs. McKinnon's words repeating in memory, "The *same*, but quieter; the *same*, but he has grown much heavenward." His human best, filled with the Holy Spirit!

That human best of his, composite of many homely graces and a few Yankee irritants, summed up to a total every honest man respected and almost every one loved. Physically he was like Spurgeon, "remarkably compact," weighing on an average of two hundred and eighty pounds. Dependable data upon his height show him to have been about five foot seven and a half. Some one during his thirties described his face as exhibiting "a gospel eye, and a law jaw covered with a brown beard." The picture that graces this chapter shows a *white* beard covering a jaw which, also, has given way to the *gospel*.

Strange, how little of precise detail his friends retained. I asked many, "What color were his eyes?" Dr. James M. Gray, embarrassed, finally said to me, "Well, well, sometimes I think they were gray, sometimes brown." Actually they were brown; "a soft brown, able to sparkle with fun, burn with intensity, and melt with love and emotion." While we are about it, we might as well finish this quotation from Jessie McKinnon: "Altogether he made one think of a very decided, business-like person; not polished in manner or style; simple, unaffected and lovable; having the most matter-of-fact reasons for doing the most unusual things."

It is a well worth while for this generation, having never seen Moody in the flesh, to push back the calendar forty years and reset the scene so as to visit him in his home. That was the chief reason why Deborah and I journeyed to Northfield.

Very well. Come along. Back to the gay nineties, with their ham sleeves and Gibson hats. If you should make Northfield the goal of a Centennial Pilgrimage, talk to the old-timers about Moody, the dear Mothers-In-Israel and their venerable husbands. They will fill your heart with homely appraisals that the Cacoëthes Scribendi overlooked. So we visited many who live off the hard highways on their dear, forgotten roads; talked to them upon that subject of which they never seem to weary, "Mr. Moody." That's the way they say it, "Mr. Moody"; just as if his chief function had been that of a well-beloved farm neighbor. We link together a few of these homespun tributes, and put them upon the lips of one old Yankee lay figure. We'll just let him talk for all his Northfield friends.

So, we ask him (we're walking on Main Street), "Where does Mr. Moody live?"

> "Right up the north end of Main Street, through East Northfield; big white house on the right; you cawn't miss it; but I'll go with you." (Glad he's going; we always have missed it when these New Englanders assure us we "cawn't.") "Is he home today? Surely! saw him about an hour ago driving Harry (the old sorrel) and the single seater . . . headed south like a streak toward Mount Hermon, nodding to everybody as he passed . . . drives like blazes all the time; loves it; goes back and forth to the Boys' School every day; takes Emma, his wife, out for a little drive at night. He surely likes children, and they like him . . . He's a good *neighbor.*"

(So we start walking up the sylvan Main Street. Frankly it looks quite up to California. What more could one say?)

"Does he like it here? Well, I *guess he does!* Mr. Moody doesn't care at all for big cities . . . doesn't like the ocean shore either; hear he gets seasick easily. . . Does he understand farming? Say, he knows so much about stock, and chickens and doves, he just doesn't seem like a preacher at all . . . he's smart, too; always has his wits about him for everything . . . he's brimful of fun; I had to laugh the other day at what he said about geese; said he liked to have some around; they made things lively!

"He's a great fellow! You'd think with everybody in the world running after him, he'd be stuck-up. Well, he isn't! . . just as humble as a child; thinks God won't use him if he gets the least bit conceited; this makes him do queer things; he pushes everyone else ahead in his Northfield programs, and tries to keep in the background; he seems to think we'd rather hear some outsider than *him!* It's gotten so we pass resolutions that we hear Mr. Moody at the next meeting; then he sets the time *for 6 a. m.!* Thinks no one will be there; but it's the biggest crowd they have! . . he won't let anybody flatter him . . . says right out, 'Strike me rather than praise me!'

"Oh, he's blunt all right. Gets lots of folks down on him, until they know him better. They find out after while his heart's all right; never speaks an unkind word of anyone, and won't let anyone else do it in his presence. . . Unitarian blacksmith here used to hate him . . . but Mr.

Moody didn't pay any attention to it . . . just kept on bringing Harry and Nellie Gray in to be shod. . . Now, that blacksmith *loves* him. Folks come to see he's wholesome; if he's wrong, he'll say so . . . I've seen him get right off the platform and go down and ask a man's forgiveness. . . Little fellow could never do *that!*

"Is he bossy? Sure! A man can't build three great schools with a thousand students, and have great city revivals without knowing what he wants, and pushing folks aside who get in his way . . . he lets *anybody* know where to head in. . . Tells 'em right out 'Do as you're told!' But say, there's one person who pays no attention to that,—Emma! He ends up by doing what she thinks best. She's mighty quiet, so he reads her mind most of the time. Oh, they're a fine couple!

"Say, you ought to hear Mr. Moody try to sing! Cawn't carry a tune in a basket! One time, when the choir was singing, first four lines were a bass solo . . . he speaks right up, 'What's the matter? don't the girls know the tune?'

*   *   *

"Well, here we are at the house . . . nice lawn. . . That donkey pulling the mower, Mr. Moody says, is a Jew—he comes from Palestine: therefore, he won't let him work on Saturday. . . That shaggy, fat dog? Belongs to Mr. Moody . . . just waiting for him to get back . . . he won't let him ride in the cart anymore; fell out once, which didn't do him any good . . . so he hangs around and whines till Mr. Moody gets back.

"Homey place, isn't it? Wide front porch . . . green blinds . . . cost Mr. Moody thirty-five hundred dollars back in '75 . . . pretty much run down, but he sure overhauled it . . . did lots of the work himself . . . sure beats all how nimble he is for a fat man. . .

"Big parlor . . . big living room . . . good farm kitchen . . . they keep plenty in that big cooler; nothing wrong with Mr. Moody's appetite: you ought to see how hearty he eats . . . they always keep lots of ice, too; he doesn't care for tea or coffee, but he sure goes after ice water . . . lots of us think he drinks too much of it . . . come on up these zigzag stairs.

"Here's his study . . . big room; three big windows; big fireplace, mother's picture over it . . . fine view of the valley, isn't it? You see, two of these walls are covered with books; mostly preacher's tools; see here, he's got everything Spurgeon ever wrote! . . Yes, big table in center is where he studies; there are his favorite books—the Bible and Müller's *Life of Trust*; . . look up here at four o'clock in the morning and you'll see his coal-oil lamp burning; sticks to coal-oil lamps right through the house . . . not a lazy bone in his body . . . fine fellow!

"The dog's barking, he must be coming . . . yes, there he is, driving like the wind . . . you say he looks rather funny? Say, when he's dressed in those yellow tweeds, and with that black velveteen coat, his folks tell him he looks like a big bumble bee! . . But you ought to see him in rainy weather; wears rubber boots right into the chapel; split up the back so he can get his legs in. . .

"No, he doesn't dress that way out in meetings . . . pretty fussy about the fit of his dark Cutaway and Ascot tie . . . thinks these hide his size. . .

"He hates expensive things for himself. Always goes to the less expensive hotels. . . He could be a rich man today, but he gives everything away. A woman gave him a thousand-dollar diamond because her son was saved. He sold it and put the money right into a Y. M. C. A. building. Does that way all the time![1]

"Here he comes . . . watch out, he's always playing jokes, full of fun . . . but mind you don't play any jokes on him! And say, never call him 'Reverend.' He hates it. Never would be ordained . . . says Spurgeon was always plain 'Mister' and that's good enough for him. He's a great fellow!"

*　　*　　*

Ah, my friend, if you can go up to Northfield before the old-timers have vanished, you will get divine heartburn to hear them talk of "Mr. Moody," just as if he died yesterday! They don't make a paragon of him; they just love him. They tell you

[1]Charles R. Erdman states that Moody thoughtfully provided for his wife, but died with only $500 in bank assets.

in so many words that he was what he was just because he was *good, harmless and undefiled.*

*   *   *

After these men and women of yesterday's world had talked to us thus for several days, we went into the big auditorium on the Northfield Campus. Memory and imagination, which give roses in December, caused him to appear seated once again on the big platform; bent head, looking at the floor, while Sankey sang. A young English girl (Helen McKay) watched that pose for months, then wrote, "I see he is asking for Guidance at every step; and he gets it." Another said: "After I'm with him a while, it's Christ I think of, not Moody. He's such a plain person; but I soon forget that, too."

There you have it–his human best, filled with the Holy Spirit! That was all there was to him. But that was enough. We catch this priceless secret in his cheery laugh when R. W. Dale in the beginning said, "I see no real relation between you and what you have done." "Oh, Doctor Dale, I'd feel very sorry if you did." But Dale and his colleagues didn't say such things twenty years later. There was a subtle change in the man; he was the same–but–the same, only he *had grown much heavenward.* The human in him had lessened in power. Self was now far away and out of ken. Somehow one couldn't be with him half an hour without becoming conscious of–Another!

XXIII
And Is Compassed About by a Cloud of Witnesses

What small values accrue from a man's superficial credentials,-his academic, social and political chits! Especially in Christian leadership. There, nothing much matters save that Evangel becomes humble clay for the Exceeding Treasure; and when he does, he is accepted-on-sight. So long as time lasts, the Glowing bush will never cease to be *the* attraction that captures the eyes of the world. Men like Moses warm their hands and fire their hearts by means of such instruments; but more important, they borrow power through which their own Egyptian deliverances are effected.

But, if Evangel *fails* of the Accolade of Heaven, the Spencerian niceties of his Latin vellums impress no one,-save himself. The multitudes from commercial Galilee, aristocratic Decapolis, scholarly Jerusalem, sterling Judea and cosmopolitan trans-Jordania, did not begin following even the Beloved Carpenter,-until *after* He was led up of the Spirit!-*Sketch Book.*

AND IS COMPASSED ABOUT BY A CLOUD OF WITNESSES

There is no doubt that the Commoner of Northfield wielded a first-line world leadership in the latter half of the nineteenth century. This was no ordinary circumstance when we remember that it was an era of unusual significance; and furthermore, that it was a time of great religious leaders, such as Maurice and Martineau, Manning and Newman, Brooks and Bushnell, Beecher and Drummond, Channing and Clark, Robertson and Fairburn, Parker and Spurgeon. In the midst of these mountain men, Moody suffered no loss of visibility. He could not be hid.

Dale was frankly perplexed about it; to him Moody was not the kind of leader he was expecting, nor did he see anything in him that explained his power. Of course, Moses could likewise have easily been puzzled over the Sinaitic miracle, *had he eyes for only the bush*. At the beginning of this research, I started to compile a "Moody's Who's Who": the men who were attracted to him, and who upheld his hands. Today the roster is so vast, it must be handled with a severe eclecticism that deals not so much with men as with principles.

There was one group, already giants when Moody attracted attention, who gave him their hearts and were profited by his spirit. Though they had but little to learn from him, they were willing to follow his leadership and become his coworkers. Such were John Kelman, (Bishop) J. H. Vincent, William Morley Punchon, Henry G. Weston, the two Bonars, Alexander Duff, Thomas Guthrie.

There was another group, of about his own age, who though head and shoulders above him as scholars, received life's most significant impulse from his illumined personality. Of such were Henry Drummond, J. E. Studd and Theodore Cuyler. Typical of this group were the saintly F. B. Meyer, who came to his own deeper experience through Moody, and Henry C. Mabie, who derived from Moody his tremendous approach to the subject of faith through the surrendered will.

And still another group. There were hundreds of prominent business men, so impressed with his merit and high purpose as to give him not only great money sums, but their own active service, such as Richard C. Morse, J. B. Stillson, John Wanamaker, Cyrus McCormick, Sam Sloan, Morris K. Jessup, R. K. Remington, W. E. Dodge, John V. Farwell, C. F. Jacobs, Peter McKinnon, H. N. F. Marshall, George H. Stuart, William Reynolds, Ed Isham, S. A. Kean. Every one of the forenamed exhibits a romance of friendship worthy of chapter-length treatment.

The story of Charles G. Hammond[1] is typical. Hammond, who died in the vice-presidency of the Pullman Company in 1884, was an outstanding Christian executive. He first met Moody in 1858,

[1]Letter of Carl Nyguist, Secretary-Treasurer, Chicago, Rock Island and Pacific, March 7, 1936.

shortly after he was made head of the Chicago, Burlington and Quincy Railroad. He became so attached to Moody that, in his own estimate, he had to "warm his heart and clear his brain by a weekly contact with D. L." All through his career, as head of the Union Pacific, then of the Pullman Company, his heart followed Moody in every move he made.

An entirely different stratum is represented by certain underprivileged boys in Moody's Bible School, who became laymen of high distinction. Typical of this group is the romance of a ragamuffin who climbed up to the station of Postmaster of Chicago. And then there were certain men of "the criminal class" who, finding Christ through Moody's gospel, were made finer than fine gold. Where is there a more remarkable narrative than that of Valentine Burke of St. Louis? This "stir-bird" saw a newspaper report of one of Moody's sermons under the title "How the Jailor of Phillipi Was Caught," and thought it referred to the jailer of Phillipi, Illinois–whom he hated. And when he found out the article was nothing but a preacher's sermon, he, in an insane rage, jumped up and down on it in his cell. But it was too late! Valentine Burke had been "caught" by the oft-repeated expression, "believe on the Lord Jesus Christ, and thou shalt be saved!" When he had been released, officers of the law–slow to believe at first–had it proven to them that Burke was a changed man, finally to be trusted in every possible way.

There was another group of powerful Christian leaders, his close friends, who felt somehow D. L.

was a mystic center of power for his age. Of such were
Henry Clay Trumbull, D. W. Whittle, C. I. Scofield,
Arthur T. Pierson, George F. Pentecost, John B. Gough,
Brownlow North, L. W. Munhall. These in turn were
followed by a new race of workers, much younger than
Moody, who held him in the same esteem, such as A. C.
Dixon, W. J. Erdman, G. Campbell Morgan, J. Wilbur
Chapman, John McNeill, George C. Needham. Strong
Christian workers arose from Moody's meetings as if by
magic, such as James Morrison, sailor evangelist; George
Sims; Charles M. Morton, the flaming associate of Henry
Ward Beecher; and the powerful pastor-evangelist
J. Wilbur Chapman, who in his senior college year had his
world turned upside down by Moody.

Almost limitless was the influence that Moody as an
older man exerted on young collegians. There was John R.
Mott, whose life found a new center of gravity through
hearing Moody, during student days at Cornell. Moody
could well put one hand on Fletcher Sims Brockman and
say to the Y. M. C. A., "I gave you this great leader"; and
the other on Adoniram Judson Gordon and exclaim to the
Baptists, "He found himself under my ministry." He could
point to John Kenneth Mackenzie and say to Chinese
Medical Missions, "He is my boy!" In Philadelphia today is
that Lake Forrest graduate, George Thompson Brown
Davis, promoter of world-wide revivals, who so fell under
the sway of Moody that his whole life was colored, and at
the age of twenty-six (in 1899) wrote one of the
outstanding biographies of Moody. And Melvin E. Trotter,

Saint of the Slums, whose soul was fired through living in Moody's room in Northfield and pouring for several years over Moody's manuscripts: "What inspiration they were to me! all in his own handwriting, many misspelled words . . . but, I loved them so very much!"[2]

More fascinating still is it to see how talented, self-sufficient youngsters were melted like wax in Moody's presence, and were glad to fit into his program. Of such was that young Irishman A. P. Fitt, law student of Limerick and Dublin. When Moody said, "I want you to hitch on with me," Fitt promptly "hitched." He became an invaluable worker in Chicago and Northfield, married Moody's only daughter, and was undoubtedly the John of Moody's heart. He colabored with Paul Dwight Moody, D. L.'s son, now president of Middlebury College, Middlebury, Vermont, in writing that popular *Shorter Life of D. L. Moody.* Mr. Fitt is today associated with the Westminster Choir School of Princeton, New Jersey. Then there was the excellent young woman, Evelyn Hall, glad to give herself to carry out D. L.'s ideals of a school "having evangelical fervor, with no scholastic abridgement." She served until 1911, a period of twenty-eight years, as preceptress of the Northfield Seminary. There was, too, brilliant Emeline Dryer, forerunner of Bible Institute, of whom we have already spoken.

It was a great race of men whom Moody selected and attached to his institutions. We close this chapter by mentioning two of them as typical of the

[2]Letter of Mel Trotter to author, March, 1936.

entire group. There was Reuben Archer Torrey who first met D. L. in 1878, at the close of his senior year in Yale. "He was a revelation to me, changing my entire conception of the Christian ministry, shaping my whole future." And when Moody said to Torrey, "Hitch on," the brilliant, exacting scholar poured the best years of his life into the Bible Institute and the Moody Memorial Church.

And there was James Martin Gray, young Church of England clergyman, who was proud to put his deep spirituality, rare scholarship and splendid executive abilities behind Moody's scheme of things, until he outdid Moody himself. His was an apostolic succession that ran for thirty years, until God called him into rest, September, 1935.

Time fails us to say more. Yet there is still another group of men who were too young to know Moody very well, but were moved as on the tide of the sea just by hearing him, or who never saw him at all, but have been transformed by sensing the after-glow of his ministry. Of such is Henry Allan Ironside, present pastor of the Moody Memorial Church. In the quiet of his study last July he told me with deep emotion his own life story. He was a western boy. Moody held meetings in Los Angeles, in a building where the Temple Baptist Church now stands. It was a temporary affair, with great wooden trusses. One truss was almost directly over Moody. Young Ironside, then about twelve, crawled out on that truss night after night, away above the crowd, to "see and hear D. L. from that lofty perch, right over him." It was Bethel for Ironside. On that high beam, he wept and prayed, "Oh dear God, please let me be a preacher, and preach to crowds just as Mr. Moody does." How mysterious the providence of the King. There is Ironside today in Moody's pulpit, wearing Moody's mantle. And wearing it with uncommon grace, be it said.

The curious thing that happened to men when they heard Moody preach was what Moses sensed when he regarded the burning bush. They seemed to distinguish in Moody's voice the voice of God commissioning them: "Come *thou*, therefore. I will send thee to Pharaoh, and I will be with thee!"

XXIV
HE GOES UP TO JERUSALEM
(April 15-25, 1892)

Now the citizens of a Proud City by the Lake did plan a Fair, so that millions of people, from every nation under heaven, might be allured to come. Then did Pilgrim have a great vision: that of flashing Redemption's bright light into the faces of these visiting multitudes. One night, as his own feet pressed the streets of the earthly Jerusalem, he saw the full glory of this Apostolic Strategy, and pledged himself, body and soul, to copy it. Alas! he soon foreswore this dream; a learned person filled him with misgivings as to the welfare of his body. But the Holy One promptly brought him into such perils of the deep that he cried, "Oh Lord! do but spare me, and I shall not be disobedient, cost what it may."—Sketch Book.

HE GOES UP TO JERUSALEM
(April 15-25, 1892)

This chapter and the next deal with the conception and performance of the greatest evangelical enterprise in Moody's career, The World's Columbian Exposition Revival, 1893. Since this was the climax of his ministry, regimenting his institutions and his life experience, it is made the climax and conclusion of this book.

As early as 1887, leading Chicago citizens began to plan for a four hundredth anniversary of the discovery of America. Almost immediately Moody dreamed of a bold frontal attack on these multitudes with the gospel. During his third English revival,[1] 1891-1892, he enlisted a group of prominent British Christians as prospective evangelists, and his emotional confirmation on the whole scheme came to a climax during his brief visit to Jerusalem. This "heavenly vision" came nearly failing, from disobedience, as we shall see; but it was gloriously performed in the six months from May 1 to October 31, 1893. Taken together, this entire suite of events, practically overlooked by every writer save H. B. Hartzler,[2] is the most dramatic story of Moody's life.

Strangely, the possibilities of the proposed Chicago Fair made Moody think of Pentecost, the first great

[1]First revival, 1873-1875; second, 1882-1884; brief trip to the United States, summer of 1883; third, 1891-1892; brief trip to Palestine, April, 1892.

[2]Hartzler, *Moody in Chicago.*

evangelical offensive ever launched. For days, caravans had verged upon Jerusalem, until the population doubled—great human tides of decent people, and a backwash of vicious ones (just the way it would be in saloon-ridden Chicago). Now these multitudes, whether good or bad, were dramatically open to impressions; that's why they were there. How appropriate, that through God's Guidance the early church should assault them with the most sensational thing in the world—the gospel.

Pentecost's greatest result, save the coming of the Spirit, was that these visiting hordes went home and reported, not upon the bazaars, but upon the Glad Tidings of Redemption and Release. Through this strategy of Pentecost the New Force invaded the nations, "in widening circles, rolling out from Jerusalem." By the grace of God, he'd copy the thing in Chicago. If other believers in other ages struck when "curiosity-bent masses went up to Jerusalem," should Christians of this age be inert? No! a thousand times, No! Such a program had limitless possibilities. To set up a Chicago plan would be a worthy copying of New Testament evangelism, which flashed the eternal glory of God's truth into the faces of thoughtless multitudes. But, he plainly saw such a program meant colossal purpose, colossal plans, colossal power. Did he wish to pay the price? Well, he "guessed" he did.

In the midst of the third English revival an interval came in which he felt justified in accepting a standing invitation from Peter and Jessie McKinnon that he and his family visit Palestine as their guests.

The party of six—Mr. and Mrs. McKinnon, Helen McKay
(Mrs. McKinnon's sister), Mr. and Mrs. Moody and Paul
(aged thirteen)—met in Rome, April 6, 1892. They arrived
in Jaffa on Good Friday, April 15, via Naples, Port Said,
and a side trip through the Suez Canal. Then for ten days
they rejoiced in the "sacred scenes of Palestine." They
reshipped from Jaffa, April 25, returning via Cairo,
the Pyramids, Florence, and Switzerland. At Basle the
party broke up, the McKinnons continuing in their
private yacht to the Fjords of Norway, the Moodys
returning to London.

Men who love Moody cannot help feeling gratitude
toward the McKinnons. They were of Scotland's best;
cultured, wealthy, humble, devout. Peter McKinnon was
head of a great steamship company. The McKinnons first
met Mr. and Mrs. Moody when they were "newly weds,"
during the Scotch revival of 1873. From then on they
were devoted friends, showering him with every comfort;
putting at his disposal their big white yacht, the *Oriental*;
giving large sums to his institutions. Jessie McKinnon had
the gift of writing Elysian prose. Her book *Recollections of
D. L. Moody*, printed for private circulation, is beyond
doubt his finest spiritual interpretation.

The limits of this volume make extensive quotations of
her dainty narrative impossible. We append a few which
portray D. L.'s reactions to the scenic glories which he
beheld on his trip to Palestine:

"The Appian Way, with its miles of tombs and
towers, and dear Mr. Moody walking alone part of

the way, that he might go on foot by the same gate through which Paul had entered as a prisoner."

"The Bay of Naples in the westerning sun; Mont Vesuvius, cloud atop; the Isle of Capri with its blue grotto guarding the Bar. Mr. Moody looked at everything, his large mind and quick eyes taking at a glance the bearings which had cost us much labor of reference."

"The ship came to Kantara, where the Suez Canal cuts through the ancient route from Syria to Egypt. We sat up till two o'clock that we might see the place in passing. Mr. Moody was deeply moved as he thought of Joseph taking Mary and the Young Child that way. The effect of the electric lights at the bow and stern of the vessel was quite magical; the wonderful glow of colors on both sides; the dull sand of the banks made irridescent in the brilliant deck lights."

We quote certain details of the visit to Jerusalem:

"I write now in the closing days of 1899, shadowed that we see Mr. Moody's face no more. I gather up the scattered fragments of memory that lie around our visit to the Holy Land, when we trod together the streets of earthly Jerusalem. Good Friday, April 15, 1892, was a beautiful day. It was arranged that we should have a service on ship-deck. The sandy plains of Joppa came in sight at 11.30 in the morning. At four o'clock we were driving past luxuriant orange groves between great cactus hedges. At Bab-el-Wady we rested our horses. We entered Jerusalem in brilliant moonlight. We were really in the Holy City, the height of our desires realized–*with Mr. Moody!*

"Easter Sunday, April 17, was a lovely morning. We waited on the Mount of Olives. The sun rose at 5.45 over the dark hills of Moab. Mr. Moody was very quiet, gazing at everything with sympathetic spirit. 'Emma,' he said to his beloved wife, 'can you realize we are on the spot where the Lord Jesus was crucified? Let us sit here and read of the resurrection morning.' As we walked back, the morning sun made the scarlet poppies among the loose lime stones doubly brilliant. Mr. Moody said, with deep feeling, 'The path seems streaked with blood.' He preached that day on the skull-shaped hill outside the city walls. 'Oh,' he cried to those who attended, 'accept this Saviour! You, young man! and you, little boy!'"

On the night following Easter, D. L. went alone into the streets of Jerusalem. The Pascal moon flooded the narrow lanes with golden light. It seemed as if a Lovely One walked beside him, and spoke to his heart. He envisioned the teeming multitudes during Pentecost forsaking the bazaars to hear from the lips of Peter the mightier sensation of Forgiveness, Resurrection Proof and Life Eternal. For a long time he walked, his heart burning within him. Greater multitudes would soon be gathering in Chicago. Finally he sobbed, "Dear

Lord, it seems as if I'm reading the Bible for the first time; it has made everything so different, reading it here. I see what Thou dost wish of me in Chicago. And, by Thy Grace, I'll do it!"

*   *   *

But,—the high vision collapsed a few days later due to some very trying circumstances. In the first place, the death of Spurgeon, January 31, 1892, had weighed upon his heart. But when he supplied the pulpit of Metropolitan Tabernacle for two weeks in November, the full sense of his loss staggered him. He and Emma felt so sorry for Susannah; she buried her heart with her husband. One night in the Spurgeon home at Westwood Susannah tearfully gave Moody her husband's Bible, the one in which he marked down his hundreds of sermons, just as they were preached. "Take it," she said, "it's Tirshatha's own Bible. I'm sure he'd want *you* to have it." Moody's eyes were blinded with tears. When he got back to his room in London, he suddenly felt very old: just as if life were about over. Spurgeon gone! How empty the world seemed!

Within a day or so, he felt premonitions of his own physical overstrain. Friends insisted that he consult a physician. The great specialist was almost discourteously frank; he insisted that "D. L. would have to slow down; his heart was badly affected; he was now fifty-five; he had been a fool to work so hard; if he expected to live, he must walk softly." Thus, during the closing days of the London meetings Moody sorrowfully decided to give up his plan for the Chicago Exposition Revival. If he were only twenty years younger! But God's work would not suffer; there would always be fresh workers as the old ones wore out.

*   *   *

On Sunday, November 23, the McKinnons took him and his son William, in their private tender, to the German Liner *Spree*, lying off Southampton. Tearful farewells; then in a few moments the big ship with her seven hundred fifty passengers sailed out ostensibly for New York, but in reality to hold a Rendezvous with Disaster!

Before the ship had gone eleven hundred knots[3] the main crank-shaft snapped asunder with a sound like a cannon, making a great break in the hull. For forty-eight hours the vessel drifted, in a sinking condition, finally starting "to sink by the head." When hope was about gone, the S. S. *Huron*, from Quebec, miraculously appeared, transhipped the passengers, and dragged the water-logged *Spree* back into Queenstown, Ireland. Five days later, D. L. and his son sailed again, in the S. S. *Etruria*, arriving in New York December 2, 1892. On the night of December 5, when he arrived in Northfield, "innumerable lights were blazing in every town window as a token of joy that D. L. was rescued from the jaws of death."

There was a dramatic incident in this shipwreck not generally known. We quote Moody's account:

[3]From Gen. O. O. Howard's account, *The Christian Herald*, January 24, 1900.

On that dark night, the first night of the accident, he remembered how in response to the word of the London doctor, he had started home with the thought that he would not work quite so hard; he would drop the Fair plan. "Then came the crash . . . no one on earth knows what I passed through in those hours . . . my loved ones! my schools! Then I prayed 'Oh, God, if you will spare my life and bring me back to America, I will go back to Chicago and this world's fair, and preach the Gospel with all the power you give me.'"

Thus he once again committed himself to Pentecostal Strategy: was "saved by peril" from disobedience to the heavenly vision! And as soon as he gave over to doing God's will, angels came and ministered unto him. "I went to the very gates of heaven during the next forty eight hours on that sinking ship. And God permitted me to come back and preach Christ, a little longer!"

XXV
AND COPIES PENTECOSTAL STRATEGY
(May 1–October 31, 1893)

The immediate foreground of this Pacific Seaboard Parish has made an ideal cloister in which to dream of that man sent from God whose name was-Moody! Typical of the vast motions of modern civilization, are two great bridges in building; one over the Golden Gate, the other flung like a scroll from the hand of God, across San Francisco Bay. Man-spiders, working day and night, have been spinning long cables between steel towers, whose bases are awash in blue salt water, and whose summits soar above the city like El Capitans. Just now, great masses of assembled steel roadway, sullen red from the priming coats, are being up-swung from ocean barges to the lofty cables-just as if they were match boxes! And they're planning a Bridge Exposition in 1939!

It fills the heart with a queer mixture of patriotism,-and apprehension. What of tomorrow? How may that Vision come again without which the people perish? It is an outworking of Grace, that we being troubled find our eyes held watching, considering the days of old and the years of ancient time. "Has the Lord cast off? Will He be favorable no more? Hath He forgotten to be gracious?" Just to gaze fixedly upon Moody's humble, Guided life, remembering the years of the right hand of the Most High, is to bring faith's laughter upon all such misgivings,-"These are my infirmities! Our God doth continue to do wonders! His right arm is still sufficient for His people, the sons of Jacob and Joseph!" Let us dare meet *our own day* with Pentecostal Strategy!-*Sketch Book.*

AND COPIES PENTECOSTAL STRATEGY
(May 1–October 31, 1893)

During the closing days of his last British campaign, 1891-1892, he preached in more than one hundred places, averaging three to four times a day. He constantly referred to the work he proposed to do in Chicago, and pleaded for the support of united prayer.

In the spring of 1892, after returning to America, he gathered the students and teachers of Northfield and Mount Hermon at six in the morning, "to seek the anointing of the Holy Spirit." [1]

"If you think anything of me, if you love me," he said with choking voice and tear-filled eyes, "pray for me that God may anoint me for the work in Chicago. I want to be filled with the Spirit, that I may preach the Gospel as never before. We want to see the salvation of God as never before."

Thus he began the copying of apostolic strategy with emphasis upon prayer; prayer for the Holy Spirit. If prayer groups may be likened unto fiery altars, then the earth must have appeared as a starry heaven; men all over the globe began daily to intercede for D. L. Not only so, but during the Fair special days were set aside for humiliation and prayer. At these times "the prayers uttered aloud

[1]Henry B. Hartzler, *Moody in Chicago.* A most valuable book, and the chief source of material in this chapter. Hartzler was at one time (1890-1895) instructor at Mount Hermon; later pastor in Pennsylvania; deceased, 1905.

311

in English, Swedish, German and other tongues sounded like Pentecost indeed."

D. L. arrived in Chicago to begin the great enterprise May 3, 1892. He had already conceived it as a vast and complicated scheme of daily meetings, all over the city; using every type of meeting-place, church edifices, empty store buildings, theaters, five large tents, gospel wagons. Likewise, he had already lined up powerful Christian speakers in England and America. "This is why I have asked these brethren to come amongst us. They have been greatly used of God. That's just what we want right here in Chicago."

There were twenty-four great American ministers of the stamp of P. S. Henson, James H. Brookes and W. G. Moorhead: twenty-five famous American evangelists, as D. W. Whittle, Merton Smith, and L. W. Munhall; a company of "anointed minstrels" like unto H. H. McGranahan, Geo. C. Stebbins (of course Ira D. Sankey); college leaders, teachers of whom C. A. Blanchard of Wheaton was a type; outstanding Christian leaders, such as Robert E. Speer, Henry Clay Trumbull; and an army of witnessing laymen, such as John G. Woolley, Stephen Merritt, Major-General O. O. Howard. Nearly forty Great Hearts came from Europe to help; we mention as types John J. Paton, John McNeill, Henry Varley, Thomas Spurgeon (C. H.'s son), Theodore Monod of Paris. And hundreds of "lesser lights," devoted laymen, pastors, musicians.

The chief sector of his army of invasion, however, was the fellowship Chicago Avenue Church and the lusty young Bible Institute. Especially the latter: "They were a capable, ready, willing body, always at command of the leader, whether for speech, song, prayer or–*to serve tables.*" He afterwards made a statement as to how well disciplined his army was: "If there was any part of the city where we needed to throw a detachment, we had them at our command. If we had only six hours' notice, we could send fifty men over to that part of the city and placard and ticket a whole neighborhood and fill a building."

There was a curious circumstance in the World's Fair Gospel Campaign: Moody was never, in any meeting of Chicago ministers or laymen, appointed or asked to head up the work! He was so obvious that such a formality was unnecessary. His years of specialized training, world-wide acquaintance with great men, universal love and confidence, unique and powerful local organizations, made his leadership so obvious that no one ever thought of passing a resolution.

Let's have a look at the Chicago of 1893. It had nearly two million inhabitants. (Naturally the Chamber said two and a half.) It had grown metropolitan; was not dismayed to say it had "fewer churchgoers in proportion than any American City." There were the same Vanity Fair, upholstered-portly-lady aspects about it as in 1934–The Century of Progress. And the same tawdry things for visitors to see–burlesque (strip variety), speakeasies, booze joints, night clubs, gambling palaces behind steel doors, gangsters, ward politicians, hop heads, yen hockers, male pansies, and street ladies-a very naughty, Big Bad Babylon, wearing its fancy exposition as Top Hat and Tails. It appeared to be a hopeless quest to get any hearing for Faith in such a Midway Plaisance.

*   *   *

But-remember, the approach Moody dreamed was to be Pentecostal Strategy! Basically, there were certain hardheaded Yankee factors in this strategy. The advertising, for instance, outspeared Wrigley. "You need not think," said D. L., "that we are going to get audiences for the asking. I know the district well, and I know that the working men don't get to bed till one or two a.m., and they are not coming to an eleven o'clock meeting without some pressure. If we want an audience, we'll have to go out and get it, and that means work." *The one great subject of the Exposition* meetings was constantly kept before the public at an average cost of over five hundred dollars per day-ads in newspapers, street cars, bill-boards; ticket passers, circulars, posters. (One firm printed half a million tickets!)

The strategy included proper places of meeting. The chief center was Haymarket Theater, seating three thousand, on West Madison Street. Here, Sunday morning services were held throughout the Fair, Moody preaching each Sunday, save two. Old Haymarket became as well known throughout the world as The White City, itself. In addition to this theater, seven others were used; also Central Music Hall and the Grand Opera House; in addition, Turner, Pullman, Columbian, and four other halls; moreover six large auditoriums; all Chicago and Englewood Y. M. C. A.'s; and the edifices of twelve Presbyterian, eight Congregational, nine Baptist, thirteen Methodist, and thirteen smaller denominational buildings. These together with tents, etc., made a grand total of over eighty meeting places, as many as seventy being used in one day!

The financing of this giant enterprise was a miracle of faith. Moody always felt sure that where God guides, He provides. Sometimes the situation became critical; but was always relieved at the right moment. One day, in Northfield, saintly A. J. Gordon felt guided to take up an offering "to help Brother Moody." The ten thousand dollars raised came just in time to prevent disaster. D. L. wrote, "I cannot tell how grateful I am to those who raised it. But, I recognize it, not as coming from them, but from the Lord."

The strategy was Pentecostal in its provision for keeping the workers up to a lofty personal level. Moody insisted that concurrent with the public evangelistic services, there should be meetings for deepening the spiritual lives of the workers. "Ah (he said) we cannot lead others nearer to Christ than we are living ourselves, and there is no use working unless we are filled with the Holy Spirit. We want to get down on our faces and humble ourselves at His feet. Let Him search us and try our thoughts, and see if there be any wicked way in us. If we do these things then our preaching will be with power, and our work will bear a precious harvest of souls." And there was the strategy of Pentecost in the theology of the meetings. D. L. saw to that! "Let's not spend time splitting hairs in theology and wrangling about creeds. Let's go to work and save lost souls. Our Gospel is the only hope of the drunkard, the gambler, the harlot, the lost on the streets of Chicago. Oh, let us go and save them! I would rather save one soul from death than have a monument of gold reaching from my grave to the heavens!"

* * *

The big offensive moved off the first Sunday morning in May at Haymarket Theater. It was S. R. O.—from floor to ceiling! and seventy-five to eighty per cent, were men! D. L. preached on "Herod and John," murderer and martyr. Over two hundred followed him to an inquiry room which was a city block away.

The siege guns—the other eighty meeting-places —started firing Sunday night. Within four weeks the currents of revival were running with torrential power. Thirty to forty thousand attended on an average each Sunday, other thousands during week nights. Sometimes the attendance was even greater: the last Sunday in August, 51,000; Sunday, September 17–62,000; the second Sunday in October, 71,000! Critics began to say, "Big crowds, sure! But they're not reaching the visitors." Moody promptly made a public test in Haymarket. Of three thousand present, twenty-eight hundred were visitors! And the critics had no more to say.

* * *

There were circumstances so dramatic that they now form pages in the Romance of Evangelism.

The Campaign for instance "beat a circus!" Forepaugh's Mammoth Circus, with a tent seating ten thousand, with room for ten thousand more in the arena, announced performances for two Sundays in June. Moody secured the tent for religious meetings for Sunday mornings. The management laughed at him. But the tent was jammed full the first service. The circus crowd in the afternoon was so small that further Sunday performances were abandoned!

On the second Sunday morning, it was so hot, with the sun beating on the canvas, "it seemed as if we all might die." Eighteen thousand people stood beneath the blistering heat, "sweat rolling down their faces, listening to a voice." "D. L. seemed like an angel of God as he spoke in the midst of the ocean of faces on the rickety center platform. The mob roar hushed; it forgot the heat; the silence became intense; Pentecost came down, and hundreds were saved!"

The Campaign "Beat the Labor Day Celebration"! Central Music Hall had been engaged for a daily, two-hour noon meeting, beginning *on Labor Day!* The streets were filled with blaring bands and pressing multitudes. Workers went into the big hall with misgivings. But they were mistaken. For two hours the power of God came down on a building packed full, and each day following it was filled, "the foaming waves of worldly traffic beating against walls within which a host of worshippers waited upon the Lord."

And as he said, when he arrived upon the ground, "We shall beat the World's Fair." On the great day of the Exposition, Chicago Day-Fire Anniversary-even the theaters dared not open, assuming everybody would be at the White City. But D. L. hired the Central Music Hall, five miles down-town from the Fair Grounds, for a continuous meeting from 9 a.m. until 6 p.m. It was continuously jammed. Torrey said, "If I hadn't climbed in a back window, they would have lost their speaker!"

And "beat the Fair" they did, it had to close Sundays for want of attendance!

But the most dramatic circumstances of the Chicago Campaign were the blessed meetings held every night, when the "tired co-workers gathered together from the scores of meeting-places to confer with Moody in his room at the Bible Institute." Like a general, he shaped his maneuvers for the next day, "catechising the workers, breathing confidence into them, taking advantage of unusual opportunities, correcting defects, hearing reports of victory, yea, and of reverses, also! Men looked back upon those late hours, lasting sometimes beyond midnight, as the Holy of Holies. They reached Moody's room 'tired to the bone'; they went out 'with strength renewed as the eagles.'"

*　　*　　*

We venture to report upon the details of a certain service, to exhibit the power-secrets for those who would like to copy in after years; it is fairly typical:

This meeting began with a "build up" song service of twenty minutes, that "roused and kindled all hearts." The items in the "build up" section were: Four songs by the congregation, led by a powerful chorus choir, accompanied by instruments; two female solos (congregation joining on one chorus); three songs by three quartettes, two male, one female; one hymn by a great male choir; three short prayers intermingled.

"The service had an upward movement like the swell of a wave," . . minds and hearts were opened to the Word. The entire service ran seventy-five minutes, embracing ten songs, five prayers, D. L.'s earnest words on the Bible, "full of fire and energy," concluding remarks by A. B. Simpson, "that fell like dew upon the hearts of the audience," and the invitation, exhortation, Amen!-"and no man felt it to be longer than thirty-five minutes!" Somebody said, "Church services ought to move like a Radio City broadcast." Of course they should! But the Connecticut Crooner, in his palmiest days, never put over "a program of matched parts" equal to the swift, fiery, soul-stirring movement of the services in the World's Fair Gospel Campaign.

Moody's entire offensive assumed that the gospel witnessed to by the Holy Spirit was the most sensational thing in the world! "Oh my friends," he said a score of times, "the right way to conquer the world's attraction is not by violence, not by law, not by threatening, but by a big enough counter attraction. Something Better!"

A typical example of his confidence in the gospel as "Something Better" flashed forth in his remarks upon renting the vast Tattersall's Hall, capacity 15,000, "We've got something better than Buffalo Bill, and we must have a bigger audience." And he did!

And he knew also that there was nothing of the "Something Better" in the New Theology. He laughingly told about the big blare made over the "Congress of Religions, . . rental of Columbus Hall, . . visions of thousands in attendance, . . then when the Big Hour came, the curtains were drawn aside and the committee faced an audience of *sixteen women and two men!*"

No man can estimate the influences of the World's Fair Gospel Campaign. We forebear giving the wild statistical guesses; they are not up to reality. Of course there were thousands of conversions. But, Moody felt something else happened more important still:

> "Christians came to Chicago from all over the world . . . many received the baptism of the Holy Spirit . . . others were stimulated . . . and fires of revival have been kindled everywhere."

*   *   *

It was long past midnight, the early morning of November 1, 1893. The great Fair had passed into history. Moody remained alone in his room after the workers had departed from their last conference. The weariness that comes when a task is over covered him like a cloud. Yet, there was a song in his heart! He felt as if his Lord was saying "Well done!"–*to him. To him!* who was so unworthy, so deficient. He sobbed aloud, and fell upon his knees beside his bed, "Oh, my Dear Lord, after these wondrous days, I'm so grateful Thou didst not let me disobey the heavenly vision! I thank Thee for the shipwreck! The old gospel has lost nothing of its power! And it never will! Dear Lord, I can say tonight with Simeon, 'Now lettest Thou Thy servant depart in peace for mine eyes have seen Thy Glory!'"

WINTER VIEW OF BIRTHPLACE

(Washburne Collection. Taken, February 5, 1920)

The heavy days of December passed over the stricken man. With tired eyes, he looked out toward the strangely transformed house where he was born, and where his mother had died. What wonders God had wrought since it stood unpainted in a barren pastureland. Today, calmly amidst the giant maples, it rested as a cherished shrine on the south line of the Seminary Campus. Somehow, the house symbolized just what had taken place in his own life-a humble vessel infilled with beauty and honor. His human best, filled with the Holy Spirit. And he understood, through Witness borne to his heart, that the King considered it to be sufficient.

XXVI
"And Comes to the Gates of Glory"
(December 22, 1899)

"In this period he had a dream, which, though he had no turn at all for taking notice of dreams, yet made a very strong impression upon his mind. He imagined that he saw his blessed Redeemer, on earth, and that he was following Him through a Large Field, following Him whom his soul loved, till he came up to the gate of a burying place, when turning about He smiled upon him in such a manner as filled his soul with the most ravishing joy, and on after reflection animated his faith in believing that whatever storms and darkness he might meet in the way, at the hour of death his glorious Redeemer would lift up upon him the light of His life-giving countenance."–Philip Doddridge, *The Life of Col. James Gardiner.*

AND COMES TO THE GATES OF GLORY
(December 22, 1899)

When Moody walked out into the streets of Chicago on the morning of November 1, 1893, leaves of hammered bronze from the boulevard trees raced along the sidewalks, driven by a chilly blast from Lake Michigan: An overture of winter! And he never did care much for winter. It made one think. He always "pushed the calendar" in the fall, looking forward to the arrival of December 21. That was a high day with him: "The back bone of *winter* is broken!" His family would reply, "But, father, winter has just started!" "Yes, I know: I know. But–the days are getting longer and spring will soon be here!"

It was a far cry, he thought, as he walked along, back to that remote September day nearly thirty years ago, when he "a green lad" had arrived in Chicago. How the city had grown! La Salle Street was "stretching out toward Wisconsin," and thousands of new homes were being erected in the shore-bordering Woodlands. Yes, the city has grown almost beyond belief–a curious constriction seized his throat. Yes, and so had he! The Lovely One who lived in his heart had so vastly transformed him, and honored him! Dear Lord, how romantic these years had been! It just made him want to weep and prayed to have seen it proved in his own life that all God needs is one's humble human best, filled with the Holy Spirit!

The morning mail brought a sheaf of interesting letters; invitations running ahead for months, yea years; invitations of cities united in their desire to have him hold meetings. How long could this continue? Well, *not long!* Men couldn't ordinarily reach threescore and ten who'd lived as dangerously as he. And he was now nearly fifty-seven! But, he'd go as far and as fast as he could, and as long as his King wished.

*   *   *

The months went by swifter than the leaves of that Autumn day in 1893. In the fall of 1899, he suddenly felt "a poignant premonition"; no better words can be found for it than these, it was the homing instinct of the soul!

Well, what difference did it make? He had fought a good fight; kept the faith; and so many loved ones were gone. "Dear Drummond! how he missed him; it just didn't seem possible he would never see him again on earth!" But the heaviest loss was the home-going of his little grandchildren. Dwight, his namesake, who lived but "one little year," before the angels took him that November day a year ago! And Irene, his first grandchild had followed her little brother just three months ago; and she only four years old! "That little child had the sweetest voice he ever heard on earth."

Dear God, he suddenly felt himself to be such an one as D. L. the aged; life lay definitely in the past. He hoped his Redeemer would forgive him; he was just an old man, lonesome for some precious things that were now Over There.

*   *   *

The Kansas City meeting was to begin about middle November. Well, he'd do his best. Should he allow his own lonely heart to interfere with his King's business? No! a thousand times, No! But the lonely heart had something to say about that! On the Sunday he started for the western city, he spoke in the Fifth Avenue Presbyterian Church, New York; spoke in a way that brought tears to hundreds of eyes: "You may read in the papers that Moody is dead. It will not be so! God has given me the gift of life everlasting."

The *Pennsylvania Limited* stopped at Philadelphia. His heart was troubled over the strange decadence of spiritual warmth in the American church. To the merchant prince awaiting him in the station he said, "When the revival spirit dies may I die with it."

*   *   *

The train rushed westward toward Kansas City. Winter was again making ready to seize the world, and he didn't care much for winter. The yellow and crimson glories of the trees beside the Wabash; the golden pumpkins and the russet corn shocks made him sob a seemingly irrelevant prayer. "Oh God, stir the cities of America again!" But, it wasn't irrelevant. He *didn't* like winter. His soul was so made that it rejoiced in spring, whether over the fields of nature or in the Church of God!

The Kansas City meeting in the mammoth Convention Hall had not gone on three days, until he knew his body was breaking. Too bad! One can't lightly give over audiences of fifteen thousand!

Then came Thursday night, November 16. Only five days out on a great campaign, and here he was obliged to give it up. But he'd do his best that last service. Wonderful, how God made his voice so strong, with him-so sick! Well, he'd use it for the King; make men ashamed of their "Excuses" for refusing His loving invitations. . . Yes, thank God, there were hundreds confessing Him.

The time had come to close the service. He leaned far out toward the vast multitudes and gave his farewell as he had given it hundreds of times in passing years. With finger uplifted, (pointing to the heavens, as did his beloved friend Spurgeon) he spoke again, *and for the last time,* his resurrection benediction, "Good night! And I'll see you in the morning!"

*　　*　　*

The hearts of thousands followed the train which bore him back to Northfield, with as much solicitude as the engineer, who began the journey at Kansas City.[1] That engineer had found Christ under Moody's preaching! Friends carried him from the train to the Homestead of Northfield; placed him in

---

[1] I was a high school boy at that time. Well do I remember the heart-felt interest of the people of my Indiana home-town.

the bedroom from which his weary eyes could gaze upon the valley scenes he loved.

The heavy days of December passed over the stricken man. With tired eyes, he looked out toward the strangely transformed house where he was born, and where his mother had died. What wonders God had wrought since it stood unpainted in a barren pastureland. Today, calmly amidst the giant maples, it rested as a cherished shrine on the south line of the Seminary Campus. Somehow, the house symbolized just what had taken place in his own life-a humble vessel, infilled with beauty and honor. His human best, filled with the Holy Spirit! And he understood, through Witness borne to his heart, that the King considered it to be sufficient.

Folks were so good to him! He and the beloved physician, Dr. Norman Perkins Wood, talked of days agone. Both of them laughed over the remote day in 1888, when the young doctor and his young wife arrived in the village to hang out their shingle. Some one had suggested, "Doc, get on the good side of Moody, or he'll run you out of town." And the young doctor replied with spirit, "Like to see him do it!" They both laughed again when they remembered how this dramatic introduction grew into one of life's sweetest friendships.

But the young doctor lost all power to laugh, when his love-vigil was broken at two a.m. on the morning of December twenty-first . . . D. L. was calling for him. The trained eyes of the physician saw the stigmata of death. . .

Loved ones with the dying man heard him say in a clear voice, "If this is death, there is no valley. This is glorious. I have been within the gates, and I saw the children! Earth is receding; Heaven approaching! God is calling me!" [2]

Then his eyes turned toward Emma⸗she who had, next to Christ, been dearest of all to him⸗and he whispered the words that sang in her bereaved heart the four lonely remaining years⸗"You have been a *good* wife to me!"

Then some one, whose handwriting we now know, wrote in that panel of the Mother's Bible headed "Deaths,"

> "Dwight L. Moody, Friday at twelve noon, December 22nd, 1899. Aged 62 yrs., 10 months, 17 days."

*   *   *

Sankey arrived in the Northfield Hotel Christmas night, the day before the funeral.

> "The saddest evening I ever spent . . . we talked of him who had been our joy in days gone by, and every now and then we would look toward the door of the hotel almost expecting to see him rush through the door . . . a great winter's storm blew down from the north . . . we waited for the morning, wondering if the storm

[2] The last words as quoted by the *Review of Reviews*, February, 1900, which are most likely historically accurate.

would break. And it did! No fairer day ever broke upon those beautiful hills than the day we buried our loved one. . . After all the addresses had been made, we carried him through the cold, frozen street, past the very door where his mother had lived and where he was born. . . We bore him to beautiful Round Top." . .

To beautiful Round Top! Lo, in the soft shadow of that June evening, in 1935, Deborah and I felt how appropriate that he and Emma should rest there. Waiting! Waiting! . . rest, just where he said he'd like to be when his Lord returned! Ours could never be the sorrow of aged F. B. Meyer who sobbed as he recalled the golden days of his yesterday, "Oh God, my world is so much thinner! Spurgeon is gone! Moody is gone! The voices are dying!"

*   *   *

No, we couldn't quite know *that* sorrow. But we could know the *same joy* which young Moody felt as he listened to young Spurgeon. "If God can use Spurgeon, he can use me!" With what excellence doth the ministry of the Commoner of Northfield prove unto us the boundless possibilities of one's humble, human best, *filled with the Holy Spirit!*

Bush Aglow!

*   *   *

Spring glory is upon my western world as this long task is finished. Heavy as it has been, I would, in view of the blessings derived, do it again, were it ten times as heavy! Spring's in my heart, too! I have eaten angels' bread, sung in the presence of God! Any pessimism affecting His power to deal with this world, hard beset though it be, seems cheap and unworthy. Our God can always bring an awakening interval! And to do this, He asks for nought else save humble servants, like unto D. L., who wait; wait, watch and pray-until the Heavenly Father fills their human best with the Holy Spirit!

*   *   *

Strangely, it seems as if certain questions keep rising up, insisting upon an answer; questions which must be answered by *myself* before this book concludes-it may be, friend reader, you can hear them, too!

"Does not the Word seem precious to you, now that you've seen how God honors it, and honors His servants who are loyal to it?"

My laughing heart replies, "More than all the world!"

"Does not Jesus appear worthy, worthy of your human best, since you've found how D. L. loved Him? Do you love Him, too?

I just want to shout, "Well, I *guess* I *do!*"

"But, do you consider your human best is enough?"

I don't try to answer *that*; my soul cries, "Oh, God! give *me* Thy Holy Spirit!"

And one last question, "What do you think of gospel preaching *now?* Do you feel it can *ever* fail? Do you want to preach anything else?"

My whole being joins in repeating a phrase, which I'm sure is caught up by the angels of God,

"No! A THOUSAND TIMES, No!"

THE END

CPSIA information can be obtained at www.ICGtesting.com
Printed in the USA
LVOW07*0341160813

348154LV00002B/3/P